DIVINELY DISTRACTED

Uprooting Lies, Planting Truth and Living Transformed"

TANYA HALL

CONTENTS

Introduction

Do you ever feel inspired during your devotional time with God, only for that moment to fade away? I understand that feeling all too well. For years, I experienced brief moments of connection with God that didn't seem to sustain me through the challenges of daily life. I longed for something more—a deeper, lasting transformation.

What if we could take the truths God reveals to us and allow them to take root in our hearts and minds, shaping every part of our lives?

Divinely Distracted is about moving beyond fleeting inspiration. It's about learning to retain what God speaks to your heart and allowing His Word to become the lens through which you see your life. This book is for those who are ready to invite God into every corner of their lives and discover what it means to live fully distracted by Him—rooted, transformed, and forever changed.

Why This Matters to Me

I know what it's like to long for God's presence yet feel overwhelmed by the noise of daily life. Over the years, I've walked through seasons of spiritual growth and struggle, learning how to take the truths God reveals and plant them deeply in my heart. I've experienced the pain of broken relationships—hurting loved ones and being hurt by them. I've felt the sting of church hurt and wrestled with where my true identity lies.

These moments led me to a pivotal realization: my worth isn't found in the approval of others or even in the church itself, but in Christ alone.

This truth brought freedom, healing, and courage. It gave me the strength to live boldly for Him and showed me that fleeting inspiration can become lasting transformation when I work with the Holy Spirit to nurture the truths God reveals. Life hasn't always been easy, but through the trials, I've learned to live with a renewed mind, rooted in God's Word.

What Qualifies Me to Write This

I'm not sharing these truths because I have it all figured out. I'm writing this because I've experienced firsthand how God can use the everyday struggles, triumphs, and quiet moments of faith to create deep and meaningful change. My journey of learning to live with a God-focused perspective has been one of trial, error, and growth. It's through these real-life experiences—and the grace of God—that I feel called to help others.

This devotional is born out of my personal journey. It's a testament to how God's truths can transform our hearts, renew our minds, and shape our lives when we allow them to take root. I'm passionate about equipping others to discover this not because I'm an expert, but because I've seen how God's wisdom, when applied daily, can change everything.

Devotional

Trusting and Knowing God

Focus Scripture

Proverbs 3:5-6

*Trust in the Lord with all your heart and lean
not on your own understanding; in all your
ways acknowledge Him, and He will make your
paths straight."*

Introduction

Trusting the Lord is more than a command—it's an invitation to a deeper relationship with God. But in order to trust Him fully, you must truly know Him. You need to know who He is, His heart, and His love for you. This isn't about following religious rituals or checking boxes off a list. It's about knowing Him personally—as your Father, your Savior, and your friend. God desires a relationship with His children, and He knows you completely. Now, He invites you to know Him just as intimately.

1

Core Message

Proverbs 3:5-6 calls us to trust in the Lord with all our hearts. It's easy to say, but how do we live it out when our own understanding gets in the way? To trust Him, you must know Him. The word "acknowledge" in this passage can also be translated as "know." *In all your ways, KNOW HIM.*

This isn't a surface-level knowing. The Hebrew word for "know" here carries the weight of deep, intimate connection. That's the kind of relationship God desires with you. He wants you to KNOW HIM in every area of your life—in your fears, your hopes, your struggles, and your victories.

Knowing God transforms your heart and renews your mind. Romans 12:2 reminds us, *"Do not conform to the pattern of this world, but be transformed by the renewing of your mind."* As you spend time in His Word, your thoughts shift from worry to trust, from fear to faith. You begin to see that God's will is always good, pleasing, and perfect.

So, how do you get to KNOW HIM? You pray, you study His Word, and you listen. You ask questions like, *"What is God teaching me about Himself in this moment?"* As you seek Him, you will see His faithfulness and love unfold in every detail of your life.

Mind Shift

What is a "mind shift"? It's when God's Word changes the way you think. The Holy Spirit reveals something new about God's character or His promises, and it transforms how you view your circumstances.

Here's an example: When fear takes over, you might remind yourself, "God is my refuge and strength." Suddenly, fear doesn't have the same grip on you because you KNOW God is with you.

Take a moment: What has the Holy Spirit revealed to you today about trusting God?

Your Mind Shift

_____

_____

_____

_____

_____

_____

_____

Song Suggestion

"Oh, I Want to Know You More" by Steve Green

As you go through your day, remember this truth: God wants you to know Him. In every challenge, in every joy, He is revealing more of who He is. Take the time to seek Him and let His Word transform your mind and heart.

Closing Prayer

Father, thank You for inviting me to know You deeply and personally. Help me trust You with all my heart, even when my understanding falls short. Teach me to see You in every area of my life and remind me that Your plans for me are always good. Renew my mind through Your Word and transform my heart so that I may reflect Your love to the world. I want to KNOW YOU more, Lord. Amen.

Devotional

Soaring Through Surrender

Focus Scripture

Isaiah 40:31

"But those who wait on the Lord shall renew their strength; they shall soar on wings like eagles; they shall run and not grow weary; they shall walk and not faint."

Introduction

Have you ever felt weary, as if your strength is gone and you can barely take the next step? Isaiah 40:31 promises that when we wait on the Lord—when we trust, hope, and rest in Him—He will renew our strength. But soaring like an eagle, running without weariness, and walking without fainting doesn't happen by chance. It happens through surrender.

The Lord revealed something beautiful to me as I preached one day, my arms wide open, describing what it means to soar. In that moment, I saw Jesus on the cross, His arms stretched out wide. The connection became clear: *the way to soar is the way of surrender.* Just as Jesus surrendered Himself fully to the Father, we must offer our lives to Him if we want to experience true renewal and strength.

Core Message

What does it mean to soar? When we think of an eagle soaring, we picture freedom and effortless flight. But in the biblical sense, soaring isn't just about freedom. The Hebrew word for "soar" also means *to lift up* or *to offer as a sacrifice.*

This is where the journey of faith becomes real. To soar, we must let go of our own efforts and surrender ourselves to the Lord. It's not about striving or trying harder; it's about trusting and yielding. When we surrender our plans, our worries, and our very lives to Him, He takes what we offer and lifts us higher than we could ever go on our own.

Jesus modeled this surrender on the cross. With His arms stretched wide, He offered Himself completely for us. And because of His surrender, we have the opportunity to soar—to rise above our circumstances and experience the renewal and strength that only God can provide.

So, how do we surrender in practical terms? It starts with waiting on the Lord. Waiting isn't passive; it's an active posture of trust and hope. It means choosing to rely on Him when you feel weak and leaning into His promises when life feels overwhelming. When we wait on Him, He renews our strength.

We often feel tired and worn out because, instead of soaring, we're trying to control everything. But just like eagles, we were meant to soar. An eagle is physically too heavy to keep flapping its wings to stay in flight—that's why it must soar! In the same way, we must surrender our control and worry so that we don't become weary.

As you reflect on your own life, ask yourself: *What areas am I still holding onto? What burdens do I need to release?* Soaring happens when we stop trying to carry everything on our own and instead offer it all to the One who can carry us.

Mind Shift

- ☐ Surrender is not weakness; it is strength. When we surrender to God, we are not giving up—we are being lifted up.

- ☐ Control is exhausting. Soaring, offering ourselves to the Lord with expectation, and trust renews our strength.

Your Mind Shift

_____

_____

_____

_____

_____

_____

_____

Song Suggestion

"Withholding Nothing" by William McDowell

As you go through your day, remember that soaring begins with surrender. Stretch your arms wide, just as Jesus did, and offer everything to Him. Let Him renew your strength and lift you higher than you could ever imagine.

Closing Prayer

Lord, thank You for the promise that those who wait on You will renew their strength. I want to soar like an eagle, but I know that can only happen when I surrender myself fully to You. Help me to trust You with every part of my life and to release the things I'm holding onto. Teach me to wait on You, to hope in You, and to trust that You are lifting me up. May my life be a living sacrifice, holy and pleasing to You. In Jesus Name, Amen.

Devotional

Peace in the Midst of the Storm

Focus Scripture

Philippians 4:6-8

"Do not be anxious about anything, but in every situation, by prayer and petition, with thanksgiving, present your requests to God. And the peace of God, which transcends all understanding, will guard your hearts and your minds in Christ Jesus. Finally, brothers and sisters, whatever is true, whatever is noble, whatever is right, whatever is pure, whatever is lovely, whatever is admirable—if anything is excellent or praiseworthy—think about such things."

Introduction

Have you ever felt like you're carrying the weight of the world on your shoulders, struggling just to keep going? I know what that feels like. Life can become so overwhelming that peace seems impossible. But Philippians 4:6-8 gives us a roadmap to finding peace, even when the storm around us is raging.

This passage isn't just about avoiding worry; it's about actively surrendering your concerns to God through prayer and thanksgiving. It's about shifting your focus from the chaos to God's promises and allowing His peace to guard your heart and mind. This is a peace that doesn't make sense to the world—a peace that comes straight from the Lord.

Core Message

Years ago, I found myself in a season where peace felt like a distant dream. I claimed to be a stay-at-home mom, but in reality, I was running a medical transportation company while raising my girls and leading a MOPS (Mothers of Preschoolers) group. My marriage was struggling—my husband was going through a hard season, and we were strained both personally and financially.

I felt like a juice box with forty straws draining me at once. No matter how hard I worked, I wasn't making any progress. One sunny day, despite the bright weather, I felt like Eeyore. The sun was shining, but I was under a heavy cloud. Desperate for peace, I went for a walk and ended up at my parents' empty house. I needed stillness—a moment to breathe.

There, I noticed a box of books and picked one up titled *Emotions*. The first chapter grabbed my attention. It talked about how emotions don't dictate the outcome of your life. You can't just wait for a warm, fuzzy moment to feel better—you have to put in the work.

I opened my Bible to Philippians 4:6-8 and Romans 8:28. God spoke so clearly to me. He reminded me that He was with me in this storm and that I needed to trust Him and be thankful—not just in the big moments, but every single day. I realized that peace wasn't about my circumstances changing; it was about my heart changing.

My situation didn't change for over three years. I still had to juggle my work, ministry, and family, but I wasn't the same. God had done something new in me. I began to see joy in the little things. I brought my girls to work with me, but instead of seeing it as a burden, we turned it into an adventure. We'd spread a blanket on a grassy patch outside the office, sharing Happy Meals, laughing, and reading stories. I even started doing silly things just to make us smile—like jumping into the bathtub fully clothed during their bath time.

God's peace allowed me to embrace the chaos without being consumed by it. I learned to trust Him with the weight of my life and to focus on His goodness instead of my struggles. Philippians

4:8 became a lifeline: *Whatever is true, noble, right, pure, lovely, admirable, excellent, or praiseworthy—think about such things.* That shift in focus changed everything.

Mind Shift

Peace isn't the absence of chaos; it's the presence of God. You don't need perfect circumstances to experience His peace—you need a heart that trusts Him.

Take a moment to reflect: What is God teaching you about peace in your current season?

Your Mind Shift

_____

_____

_____

_____

_____

_____

_____

Song Suggestion

"Peace Be Still" by The Belonging Co. ft. Lauren Daigle

When life feels overwhelming, remember that God's peace is just a prayer away. It doesn't depend on what's happening around you;

it flows from trusting Him with everything. Even in the midst of the storm, His peace can carry you through. Let Him calm your heart today.

Closing Prayer

Lord, thank You for offering me peace that transcends all understanding. I confess that I often let worry and fear take over, but I choose today to trust You. Help me to surrender my concerns to You and to focus on what is true, noble, and lovely. Teach me to be thankful in every situation, knowing that You are always with me and that You are working all things for my good. Guard my heart and mind with Your peace, and help me to rest in You. God transform my mind so that thankfulness is a normal way of life. In Jesus name, Amen.

Devotional

Standing Firm in Faith

Focus Scripture

---

2 Chronicles 20:12b

*"We do not know what to do, but our eyes are
on you."*

Introduction

Have you ever felt completely out of answers, staring down a
situation that seems impossible? King Jehoshaphat knew exactly
what that felt like. Despite doing the right things—seeking God
and leading his people in righteousness—he found himself under
attack from three powerful armies. His response is both humbling
and inspiring: he cries out to the Lord and says, *"We do not know
what to do, but our eyes are on You."*

That moment of surrender—where fear and faith collide—is a
place I know well. There have been seasons in my life where I felt
overwhelmed, attacked on every side. But like Jehoshaphat, I've

learned that when I don't know what to do, the best thing I can do is fix my eyes on God.

Core Message

King Jehoshaphat's story in 2 Chronicles 20 is a beautiful reminder of what it looks like to trust God in the middle of the storm. When faced with an overwhelming attack, he didn't rely on his own strength or strategy. Instead, he gathered the people, sought the Lord in prayer, and acknowledged their complete dependence on Him.

God's response was clear: *"You will not have to fight this battle. Take up your positions; stand firm and see the deliverance the Lord will give you."* Jehoshaphat and his people obeyed. They stood firm, holding their ground, and watched as God kept His Word. He fought their battles—both the old ones and the new ones.

What struck me most when studying this passage was that God didn't just defeat their enemies; He allowed His people to plunder their attackers. What was meant to destroy them became their provision, equipping them for the next season of their journey.

This truth resonated deeply with me. There were times when I cried myself to sleep, begging God to help me stay strong, to remind me that I was loved by Him. The battle was fierce, yet God was faithful. He caused me to bear fruit even in desert places. His

Living Water sustained me when I felt like I couldn't take another step.

Now, I'm living in the plunder of those battles. God has taken what was meant for harm and turned it into good. He's used my struggles to equip me, strengthen me, and prepare me for what's next. And as I look back, I see that even in the hardest moments, He gave me joy in the midst of the storm.

Like Jehoshaphat, I'm learning to take my stand, to hold my ground, and to keep my faith in God. The enemy may press hard, but I know it's because he sees the purpose God is drawing out of me.

Mind Shift

The battle is not mine; it's the Lord's. What the enemy meant to destroy me, God will use to equip me for His purpose.

Take a moment to reflect: Where is God calling you to stand firm in faith today? What plunder might He be preparing for you through this battle? Write your mind shift here:

Your Mind Shift

_____

_____

_____

_____

_____

_____

_____

Song Suggestion

"Do It Again" by Elevation Worship

No matter what battle you're facing today, remember Jehoshaphat's prayer: "We do not know what to do, but our eyes are on You." Trust that God is fighting for you and that He will turn what was meant for harm into provision for your journey ahead. Stand firm and see His deliverance.

Closing Prayer

Lord, thank You for fighting my battles. When I feel overwhelmed, remind me to fix my eyes on You. Help me to stand firm, to hold my ground, and to trust that You are working all things for my good. I ask for Your power and wisdom, grace and strength, to do my part while I watch You do Yours and to be certain that You are at work. Thank You for turning my struggles into blessings and equipping me for what's next. God help me look for You and for the good that You are bringing through every situation. I I am Yours, Lord—freed, healed, and ready for all that You have for me. Amen.

Devotional

Just Be the Donkey

Focus Scripture

Job 39:5-6

"Who let the wild donkey go free? Who untied its ropes? I gave it the wasteland as its home, the salt flats as its habitat."

Introduction

There's something freeing about being exactly who God created you to be. In Job 39, God speaks of the wild donkey—free, untied, and fully at home in the wasteland. It's a picture of living in the freedom of His design, unhindered by the expectations or opinions of others.

This lesson hit home for me during the stillness of the COVID-19 lockdown. I found myself reflecting on my life, my purpose, and how often I had tried to wear masks or fit into molds that weren't mine to fill. God gently reminded me to "just be the donkey"—to rest in His love, abide in Him, and trust that I am fully capable of doing what He has called me to do in Him and through Him.

Core Message

I've realized how easy it is to get caught up in striving. Whether it's wanting to be recognized, proving my worth, or filling roles that weren't meant for me, I've been guilty of trying to force fruit rather than letting it grow naturally from abiding in Christ. But the wild donkey of Job 39 isn't tied down or striving to be something it's not. It thrives in the space God has given it, fully reliant on His provision.

Learning to "just be the donkey" hasn't been easy. There are moments when the old patterns creep in—like the day a pastor friend of mine led a food giveaway, and I wasn't in charge. The temptation to feel overlooked or unimportant whispered to my heart. But I knew that wasn't me anymore. God had been teaching me to find joy in being part of His work, whether I was leading or supporting. It felt so freeing to know I didn't need a title or recognition to have value.

One of the hardest lessons in this journey was stepping down from the Eastside Mission. God asked me to let it go, even though it meant losing my last source of income. It was a scary leap, but I obeyed. That obedience led to new opportunities with Always

Hope and the NOW House ministries. It was the next chapter for me—one that kept me aligned with what God had created me for.

Every step of this journey has been about learning to abide in God's love and trust His voice above all others. It's about silencing the doubts that say, *"Who do you think you are?"* and embracing the truth that God has uniquely equipped me for the life He's called me to live.

Mind Shift

1. Abide in the Vine: When we stay rooted in God's love, the fruit grows naturally. We don't need to strive or force it.

2. Trust God's Voice: Like Caleb in Numbers 13:30, we can silence the doubts and confidently take the land God has given us.

3. Embrace Who You Are: You were designed with purpose. Stop trying to wear someone else's armor or meet expectations that aren't from God.

4. Find Joy in Obedience: Even when it's scary or costly, God's plans are always better than our own.

I am fully equipped to live the life God has called me to. I'm not equipped for your calling and you are not equipped for mine. I don't need position, recognition, or approval to thrive—I just need to abide in Him.

Take a moment to reflect: Where is God calling you to rest in His love and trust His plan?

Your Mind Shift

_____

_____

_____

_____

_____

_____

_____

Song Suggestion

"Who You Say I Am" by Hillsong Worship

Remember, God created you to thrive in the space He's given you. Stop striving to be more or different. Rest in His love, abide in Him, and just be the donkey. He's got you.

Closing Prayer

Lord, thank You for creating me with a purpose and calling me to live in the freedom of Your design. Help me to abide in You, to trust Your voice, and to silence the doubts that hold me back.

Teach me to live fully as the person You've created me to be—nothing more and nothing less. Thank You for Your love, which strengthens me and fills me to overflowing. Keep me rooted in You, Lord. In Jesus Name, Amen.

Day 6

Growing Your Roots

Today is so important. Today and tomorrow's time with the Lord is what makes this devotional book different. It is what will make us different. We will look back at the last 5 days; the scripture and our mind shifts. We will write them down. Then we will ask the Lord to show us what we need to reread today. These are truths that we want to transform our minds. These seeds need to be fed so they can grow deep roots within us.

Before reading the scriptures writing your mind shifts down, lets pray.

Lord, open my heart to remember the truths You have spoken to me this week. Show me what You want me to look at again and let these truths take deep root in me. In Jesus name. Amen. \

1. Trusting and Knowing God: Proverbs 3:5-6 Trust in the Lord with all your heart and lean not on your own understanding. In all your ways acknowledge Him and He will make your paths straight.

Your Mind Shift

_____

_____

_____

_____

2. Soaring Through Surrender: Isaiah 40:31 But those who wait
   on the Lord shall renew their strength; they shall soar on wings
   like eagles; they shall run and not grow weary; they shall walk
   and not faint."

Your Mind Shift

_____

_____

_____

_____

3. Peace In The Midst of the Storm: Philippians 4:6-8 "Do not be
   anxious about anything, but in every situation, by prayer and
   petition, with thanksgiving, present your requests to God. And
   the peace of God, which transcends all understanding, will
   guard your hearts and your minds in Christ Jesus. Finally,
   brothers and sisters, whatever is true, whatever is noble,
   whatever is right, whatever is pure, whatever is lovely,

whatever is admirable—if anything is excellent or praiseworthy—think about such things."

Your Mind Shift

_____

_____

_____

_____

4. Standing Firm in Faith: 2 Chronicles 20:12b "We do not know what to do, but our eyes are on you."

Your Mind Shift

_____

_____

_____

_____

5. Just Be the Donkey: Job 39:5-6 Who let the wild donkey go free? Who untied its ropes? I gave it the wasteland as its home, the salt flats as its habitat.

Your Mind Shift

_____

_____

_____

_____

What Mind Shift has impacted you the most this last week? Summarize it here so that it I easy to find.

_____

_____

_____

_____

Closing Prayer

Lord transform me in these areas, not just for a moment but for a lifetime. I want to show the world who You are through my life and that can only happen by the power of Your Holy Spirit working in me. Lord please remind me that this is about resting in You, staying connected to You. Work in me. In Jesus name. Amen.

Day 7

Finishing the Week In Worship

As your sister in Christ and fellow sojourner—great job! You are growing in the Lord and allowing His Word to transform your heart and mind to align with His Spirit, who lives in you.

Today is our first day of thanksgiving. Take time to thank God for what He has shown you through His Word and for what He has done. Thank Him for what He is going to do in and through you. If you don't have an answer for one of the prayers, that's okay. Maybe this has been a rough week for you—let God love you right where you are.

Be sure to pray the prayer at the bottom, though. Your heart needs to be fed His loving truth and worship.

God I thank You for showing me that You are:

_____

_____

_____

_____

God I thank You for what You have done

_____

_____

_____

_____

God I thank You for what I know You are doing

_____

_____

_____

_____

Go back to your favorite songs from this week and worship!!

Closing Prayer

Lord I want to know You and see You in all the world around me. Some days I do that well and as You know some days are not so great. Thank You for loving me on this journey. Help me to spread my wings in trust to You today. You are so faithful. I lay down the things that I have picked up this week. I lay them at Your feet. I want to soar. I know I can see so much better from there. My worries I give to You. Thank You for your peace when life doesn't make sense. My eyes are again lifted to You. The battles are Yours. Thank You for fighting for me. And as I walk through this next week please keep teaching me to just be the me that You made me to be. Thank You for reminding me that I am good, very good. Not because of anything that I have done or not done, but because I am Yours. In Jesus name keep making me. Amen.

Devotional

Equipped for Your Calling

Focus Scripture

Romans 5:2

"Through Him we have also obtained access by faith into this grace in which we stand, and we rejoice in hope of the glory of God."

Introduction

Have you ever tried to fit into someone else's mold? Maybe you've compared your gifts, talents, or journey to someone else's, thinking you needed to be more like them to fulfill your purpose. In 1 Samuel 17, David's story reminds us that God equips us uniquely for the assignments He has given us.

When David prepared to fight Goliath, King Saul tried to help by offering his armor. But it didn't fit. David stumbled awkwardly, quickly realizing he couldn't fight his battle using someone else's tools. Instead, he set the armor aside, picked up his sling and stones, and stepped into the fight with what God had already given him. And that's when the victory came.

Core Message

David's story in 1 Samuel 17 is so relatable because we've all been tempted to wear *Saul's armor.* Maybe you've looked at someone else's wisdom, experiences, or gifts and thought, *"If I could just be more like them, I'd be successful."* But David's victory wasn't in trying to be Saul—it was in trusting that God had equipped him perfectly for his own battle.

The Lord showed me that we're often like David, trying to fight our battles with someone else's gear. But God has equipped each of us with unique tools, experiences, and talents. If David had gone to face Goliath in Saul's armor, he would have failed. That armor wasn't made for him. His sling and stones may have seemed small and insignificant, but in God's hands, they were more than enough.

Romans 5:2 reminds us to confidently and joyfully look forward to becoming all that God has in mind for us to be. God doesn't make mistakes. He created you with a purpose and equipped you with everything you need to fulfill it.

This isn't always easy to embrace. It's tempting to compare ourselves to others and wonder if we're enough. But when we trust

God's design and lean into His plans for us, we discover the beauty of being exactly who He made us to be.

I've had to learn this lesson myself. There were times I felt like I needed to fit into someone else's shoes to succeed—whether as a mom, a leader, or even in ministry. But God gently reminded me that He didn't call me to be someone else. He called me to be *me*. He's equipped me with my own unique experiences, gifts, and perspective, and that's enough—because *He is enough*.

Like David, we're not called to walk in someone else's armor. We're called to trust that the sling and stones God has placed in our hands are all we need. And when we do, He takes what we offer and uses it for His glory.

Mind Shift

☐ God has already equipped me with everything I need to fulfill His purpose for my life. I don't need to compare myself to others; I just need to trust Him.

Take a moment to reflect: Are you trying to walk in someone else's armor? What unique tools has God placed in your hands for this season? Write your mind shift here:

Your Mind Shift

_____

_____

_____

_____

_____

_____

_____

Song Suggestion

"Confidence" by Sanctus Real

As you go through your day, remember that God has uniquely equipped you for the battles you face. Don't try to wear someone else's armor. Trust in the tools He's given you, and confidently step into the purpose He's prepared for you.

Closing Prayer

Lord, thank You for creating me with a unique purpose. Forgive me for the times I've compared myself to others or tried to be someone I'm not. Help me to trust that You've equipped me perfectly for the assignments You've given me. Teach me to use the tools You've placed in my hands with confidence, knowing that You are enough. I rejoice in the hope of becoming all that You've called me to be. In Jesus Name, Amen.

Devotional

Keeping Promises and Watching God Show Off

Focus Scripture

Psalm 21:8

"Through the victories You gave, his glory is great; You have bestowed on him splendor and majesty."

Introduction

Have you ever made a promise to God and then let it slip to the back of your mind? Maybe life got busy, or you started to doubt whether you could follow through. I once promised God that after selling my medical transportation business so that I could be a stay at home mom, I would start a Teen MOPS group in Flint. It seemed like such a great idea in the moment, but almost a year passed, after my business had sold and I had done absolutely nothing to keep that promise.

God, however, didn't let me off the hook. Through the persistence of a friend, Christy, and His incredible faithfulness, He not only helped me fulfill that promise but also did far more than I could have imagined. This is the story of how He showed off, taught me valuable lessons, and changed my heart in the process.

Core Message

The journey started with Christy holding me accountable. She gave me two weeks to get moving, and when I hadn't, she left a pointed message on my answering machine. Scrambling to make it look like I was making progress, I set up a meeting with Flint School of Choice and scheduled an informational meeting for potential volunteers. Little did I know, God was about to blow my mind.

The morning of my meeting with the school principal, I prayed with my two little girls. We asked that the principal would allow us to use the school building for Teen MOPS after school. But when I met with him, it was clear he was in a hurry. He quickly directed me to someone else—a woman named Mrs. Yuille, who worked directly with the school's teen moms.

I sat down in her office, trying to explain what Teen MOPS was all about. Before I could even ask about using the building, she said, *"We need classes for our teen moms during 2nd and 3rd hours and 4th and 5th hours. Can you lead them?"* What? Huh?

Yes! When she asked when we could start, I confidently said, *"Two weeks,"* even though I had no idea how that was going to happen.

I left the school with two class rosters of teen moms and an overwhelming sense of awe. I sat in my car and yelled, *"God, You are in a public school!"* Then I drove to my daughters' school and pulled my daughters out of their classes just to tell them what God had done. Teen MOPS wasn't going to be an after-school program—it was going to be part of these girls' school day.

The informational meeting I had planned turned into a call to action. We had one week to pull everything together. God provided every volunteer we needed for both class periods—except for one position: the coordinator.

I told God, *"That's not my job. I'm not the girl for this."* But God knew better. From the very first day, He softened my heart, and I fell in love with those young moms.

Over the next two years, our Teen MOPS group experienced God's provision in amazing ways. The first year, the school wouldn't let us host a Christmas party because we were Christians. By the second year, they trusted us so much that they gave us a $1,500 donation from a local Catholic church and even bussed all the girls to Richfield Church for a Christmas party.

God was showing off.

Mind Shift

1. Keep Your Promises to God: Even if you feel unqualified or uncertain, God will provide everything you need when you step out in faith.

2. Hold Each Other Accountable: Christy's persistence pushed me to act, and God used her to make sure I followed through.

3. Let God Change Your Heart: I went into Teen MOPS thinking I wasn't the right person for the job. God used that experience to soften me, teach me, and show me His grace.

4. Share the Journey with Your Children: Including my daughters in the process not only strengthened my faith but also theirs. They saw firsthand how God works.

5. Remember God's Faithfulness: When life feels overwhelming, look back on the moments when God outdid Himself. Let those victories hold you steady in the storm.

God is faithful to keep His promises, and He equips us to keep ours. What He asks of us is never beyond what He can accomplish through us.

Take a moment to reflect: What promise has God called you to keep? Where can you trust Him to show off in your life?

Your Mind Shift

_____

_____

_____

_____

_____

_____

_____

Song Suggestion

"Build A Boat" by Colton Dixon

God always has us covered. He's faithful to equip us for what He calls us to do, even when we feel unprepared. Trust Him, take the next step, and watch Him show off in your life. Stay obedient— He is faithful.

Closing Prayer

Lord, thank You for being so faithful, even when I hesitate or feel unqualified. Help me to keep the promises I've made to You and to trust that You will provide everything I need. Thank You for the moments when You go above and beyond, reminding me that You are always at work. Change my heart where it needs to be changed, and help me to rest in Your faithfulness. Amen.

Devotional

Abiding in the True Vine

Focus Scripture

John 15:5

I am the vine; you are the branches. If you remain in me and I in you, you will bear much fruit; apart from me you can do nothing.

Introduction

What does it mean to be "in Christ"? It's a phrase we hear often, but its depth and beauty can sometimes be overlooked.

John 15 paints the picture beautifully. God is the Gardener, Jesus is the True Vine, and we are the branches. Our job isn't to force fruit to grow or strive to be more. Our job is to stay connected to the Vine—to abide, to live there.

Core Message

In a Bible study I'm doing, they interviewed a woman who works in a vineyard. She explained the process of grafting in a new branch, and it opened my eyes to what it truly means to be *"in Christ."*

When a vinedresser grafts a new branch into the vine, it starts as a tiny bud. That's you and me—a small bud in the hands of the Gardener. The vinedresser carefully cuts a spot in the True Vine to make room for the new branch. This process involves wounding the vine, and all of the sap—the lifeblood—rushes to that spot. The vinedresser then places the new bud into the wound, binding it tightly so that the life of the vine flows into the new branch.

What a powerful picture of what Jesus has done for us! 1 Peter 2:24 says, *"He Himself bore our sins in His body on the tree, so that we might die to sins and live for righteousness; by His wounds you have been healed."*

Through the wounds of Jesus, we are grafted into the True Vine. His blood, His sacrifice, made it possible for us to become children of God. But this isn't just a one-time event—it's the beginning of a relationship where we are invited to abide in Him daily.

To abide means to dwell, to take up residence, to live fully connected to Jesus. It's not a temporary visit—it's kicking off your shoes, getting cozy, and staying in the place where God wants you to be.

When we abide in the Vine, His life flows into us, and we begin to bear fruit that resembles Christ. But if we disconnect—if we try to live in our own strength—the branch (us) dries up. Abiding is essential.

Philippians 4:19 reminds us that God will provide everything we need through Christ. When we stay connected to Him, we can trust that He is the source of all we need: His love, His grace, His favor. Our job isn't to strive for more but to remain rooted in Him, trusting that He will do the work in us and through us.

Mind Shift

Spend Time in His Word: Let God's truth sink into your heart. John 15:7 says, "If you remain in me and my words remain in you, ask whatever you wish, and it will be done for you."

1. Stay in His Presence: Pray, worship, and simply sit with Him. Make abiding a priority, not an extra thing to do but a necessity.

2. Trust the Gardener: Know that God is tending to you, pruning and providing so that you can flourish.

3. Focus on His Love: Meditate on His grace, favor, and goodness. Let His love be the foundation of everything you do.

I don't need to strive to produce fruit. My only job is to abide in Christ, trusting Him to do the work in me and through me.

Take a moment to reflect: Where is God calling you to abide more deeply?

Your Mind Shift

_____

_____

_____

_____

_____

_____

_____

Song Suggestion

"Strength of the Lord" by Joni Eareckson Tada

Remember, abiding isn't about striving—it's about resting in who God is and what He's already done. Stay connected to the source, and watch as His life flows into you and through you. You are a new creation—live in that truth!

Closing Prayer

Lord, thank You for grafting me into the True Vine through the wounds of Jesus. Help me to abide in You every day, to live fully connected to Your love and grace. Teach me to trust You as my Gardener, knowing that You provide everything I need to grow and bear fruit. Let Your life flow through me, producing fruit that reflects Your character. Thank You for making me a new creation in Christ. Amen.

Devotional

Faithful in the Waiting

Focus Scripture

---

1 Samuel 16:13

"So Samuel took the horn of oil and anointed him in the presence of his brothers, and from that day on the Spirit of the Lord came powerfully upon David."

Introduction

What do you do when God gives you a promise, but it hasn't come to pass yet? That's a hard place to be. David's story in 1 Samuel is a powerful reminder of how to handle the waiting. He was anointed as the next king of Israel, but instead of stepping into the palace, he stayed where God had him.

This season of waiting wasn't wasted—it was preparation. David wasn't in a rush to take the throne; he trusted that God's timing was perfect. He faithfully served in the roles he was given, resting in God's presence and plan.

Core Message

In 1 Samuel 16, David is chosen and anointed to be the next king of Israel. What an incredible moment that must have been! But instead of being crowned right then and there, David continued to live the life he had before. Later, he even served King Saul by playing the harp to comfort him. He was part of Saul's staff and could have stayed with him. However, where do we find David when his father asks him to check on his brothers? He is tending the sheep (1 Samuel 17:20).

It amazes me that David, already knowing he was the future king, chose to stay humble. He didn't rush ahead or push his way to the top—he stayed faithful to the work in front of him.

What stands out most to me is how God used David's time of waiting to prepare him for what was ahead. In the fields, he learned to fight off lions and bears, skills that gave him the confidence to face Goliath. While shepherding the sheep, he learned how to place his trust in *his own* Shepherd. That battle wasn't won in the moment—it was won in the preparation. David trusted that the same God who had delivered him before would deliver him again.

David's story challenges me. How often do I want to skip ahead to the *"good part"*? How often do I grow impatient when God doesn't move as quickly as I'd like? David shows us that waiting on God isn't passive—it's active trust. It's choosing to serve where He has you, knowing that He is working all things together for your good.

Mind Shift

Faithfulness Where You Are: David didn't abandon his responsibilities because of his anointing. He trusted that God would bring the promise to pass in His timing.

1. Preparation Happens in the Ordinary: The fields and the small assignments prepared David for the throne. God often does His greatest work in the hidden places.

2. Humility Matters: David served Saul and obeyed his father, even though he knew he was chosen to be king. He didn't demand recognition or a position.

3. Trust God's Timing: David rested in the fact that God would fulfill His promise. He didn't need to strive or make it happen on his own.

The waiting is where God works in me the most. I can trust that He is preparing me for what's next, even when it feels slow or ordinary.

Take a moment to reflect: Where is God asking you to be faithful while you wait for His promise?

Your Mind Shift

_____

_____

_____

_____

_____

_____

_____

Song Suggestion

"Waiting For You" by Persistenc3

David's life reminds us that God's plans don't always move on our timeline, but His timing is always right. Stay faithful where He has you. The preparation in the waiting is part of His beautiful plan for your life.

Closing Prayer

Lord, thank You for David's example of faithfulness and trust. Help me to rest in the work You are doing in me during the waiting seasons. Teach me to serve with humility and faith, knowing that Your timing is perfect. I trust You to fulfill Your promises in Your way. Thank You for preparing me for what's ahead. In Jesus Name, Amen.

Devotional

Be Careful What You Ponder

Focus Scripture

Luke 2:19

"But Mary treasured up all these things and pondered them in her heart."

Introduction

Have you ever stopped to think about how powerful your thoughts are? Mary, the mother of Jesus, could have easily let her mind dwell on the difficult circumstances surrounding His birth. She was far from home, riding on a donkey, about to give birth in a stable with no nursemaid or family by her side. Yet Luke 2:19 tells us that Mary didn't focus on the challenges. Instead, she chose to treasure and ponder the clarifying moment when the shepherds came to worship her Son.

Mary's example challenges us to consider what we choose to ponder. What we hold in our hearts and minds shapes our outlook, our peace, and even our choices.

Core Message

Throughout my life, I've had to make choices about what I would ponder. In an emotionally abusive marriage, I could have focused on the pain, the betrayal, and the scars left behind. But instead, I chose to focus on God's redeeming hand—the way He shone light on my path and led me out. Not perfectly, but intentionally, asking God to give me that power.

It reminds me of David in 1 Samuel 17. When he stood before King Saul, preparing to face Goliath, David recalled how God had delivered him from the lion and the bear. He didn't focus on how terrified he must have been in those moments or the injuries he may have endured. He could have decided never to fight again because it was too scary.

What if he had retold the story like this? *"I saw that lion grab hold of my sheep. I was so scared. I ran and was trying to pry the sheep out of its mouth when it cut my arm with its teeth. I barely got it out. When it turned on me, I grabbed it and somehow killed it. That was too much for me. Next time, I'll just let it have the sheep. I still have the scar on my arm."*

Instead, he remembered God's power within him. That focus gave him the courage to say, *"The Lord, who delivered me from the paw of the lion and the paw of the bear, will deliver me from the hand of this Philistine"* (1 Samuel 17:37).

Like Mary and David, we have a choice about what we store up in our hearts. We can dwell on the hard parts, the doubts, and the fears, or we can focus on God's faithfulness, His promises, and His power. What we choose to ponder doesn't just impact our thoughts—it impacts our emotions, our actions, our faith, and our joy.

Mind Shift

1. Choose to See God's Faithfulness: Mary treasured the shepherds' worship as a reminder of God's plan. David remembered God's strength in past battles to prepare for the next one. What moments of God's faithfulness can you treasure in your heart?

2. Redirect Negative Thoughts: It's easy to replay the hard parts, but choose instead to focus on how God has worked through those situations. Let His light shine in your perspective.

3. Anchor Your Heart in His Promises: Holding onto God's truth steadies us in difficult seasons. Meditate on His Word and trust His plans.

What I choose to ponder shapes my life. Instead of focusing on the hard parts, I will treasure God's faithfulness and let His truth guide my heart.

Take a moment to reflect: What are you treasuring in your heart today? Where can you see God's faithfulness, even in the hard times? Write your mind shift here:

Your Mind Shift

_____

_____

_____

_____

_____

_____

Song Suggestion

"Goodness of God" by Bethel Music

The thoughts we choose to treasure will shape our hearts and guide our steps. Like Mary, choose to ponder God's faithfulness. Like David, remember His power in past battles. Be careful what you store up in your heart—it's the key to living in His peace and purpose.

Closing Prayer

Lord, thank You for the gift of Your presence in every season of my life. Help me to choose carefully what I ponder in my heart. Teach me to treasure Your faithfulness, to focus on Your promises, and to see Your hand in every situation. Thank You for being my Redeemer and my strength. Help me to walk in Your truth, no matter what comes my way. In Jesus Name, Amen.

Day 13

Growing Your Roots

1. Equipped For Your Calling: Romans 5:2 "Through Him we have also obtained access by faith into this grace in which we stand, and we rejoice in hope of the glory of God."

    ### *Your Mind Shift*

    _____

    _____

    _____

    _____

2. Keeping Promises and Watching God Show Off: Psalm 21:8 "Through the victories You gave, his glory is great; You have bestowed on him splendor and majesty."

    ### *Your Mind Shift*

    _____

    _____

    _____

    _____

3. Abiding in the True Vine: John 15:5 I am the vine; you are the branches. If you remain in me and I in you, you will bear much fruit; apart from me you can do nothing.

Your Mind Shift

_____

_____

_____

_____

4. Faithful in the Waiting: 1 Samuel 16:13

"So Samuel took the horn of oil and anointed him in the presence of his brothers, and from that day on the Spirit of the Lord came powerfully upon David."

Your Mind Shift

_____

_____

_____

_____

5. Be Carefull What You Ponder: Luke 2:19

"But Mary treasured up all these things and pondered them in her heart."

Your Mind Shift

_____

_____

_____

_____

Which of these do you feel the Holy Spirit leading you to focus on? Go back and reread that devotional today. Let that new truth begin to grow within you, transforming your thinking. Write anything you need to remember about it below.

_____

_____

_____

_____

Closing Prayer

Lord thank you for time with You in Your Word this last week. Thank You for the new mind shifts that are helping me to think more and more like You. Thank You for equipping me with everything I need for what You have called me to do. Lord You do give us the desires of our hearts. Sometimes they look so much different than we thought but truely You satisfy us. As I continue to abide, live and dwell in YOU, feed me so that fruit is produced in me. Keep me content like David was in the fields shepherding the sheep, even when I want to move on. You use every day to prepare us for where You are taking us. And please check me when I am getting distracted, ahead of myself or treasuring up burdens instead of blessings. I want to ponder Your wonderful work in my life and those around me. Even in nature Lord show me who You are. I am Your Servant and I am listening. In Jesus Name amen.

Day 14

Finishing the Week In Worship

Today will be our 2nd day of Thankfulness. Take time today to thank God for what He has shown you through His Word and for what He has done. Take time to thank Him for what He is going to do in and through you. If you don't have an answer for one of the prayers that is ok. Maybe this has been a rough week for you. Let God love you right where you are. Be sure to pray the prayer at the bottom though. Your heart needs to be fed His Loving Truth and Worship.

God I thank You for showing me that You are:

_____

_____

_____

_____

God I thank You for what You have done

_____

_____

_____

_____

God I thank You for what I know You are doing

_____

_____

_____

_____

Go back to your favorite songs from this week and worship!!

Today we will close with a place for you to draw, doodle or write words that the Holy Spirit is bringing to your mind. Draw below or scribble anything that comes to mind.

Closing Prayer

Lord I am so thankful that I know You. I am thankful to know You more. Keep making me the me that You purposed me to be and I will do my best to stay pliable in Your Hands. In Jesus Wonderful Name, Amen.

Devotional

Quiet the Voices

Focus Scripture

---

2 Timothy 1:7

"For the Spirit God gave us does not make us timid, but gives us power, love, and self-discipline."

Introduction

Life is full of voices. Some encourage us, while others question our motives, belittle our faith, or magnify our fears. How we respond to these voices determines whether we move forward in faith or shrink back in doubt.

David and Caleb both faced moments where they had to tune out the noise to follow God's call. Their stories remind us of the power of focusing on God's truth while silencing the distractions around us.

Core Message

In 1 Samuel 17, David is sent by his father on a mission to check on his brothers, who are in the midst of a standoff with the Philistines. When he arrives, he hears Goliath's taunts and begins asking about what will happen to the man who defeats the giant. This catches the attention of his older brother, Eliab, who accuses David of being conceited and irresponsible.

David doesn't argue with Eliab or let his brother's words shake him. Instead, in 1 Samuel 17:30, *David turns away.* He doesn't let Eliab's voice define him or distract him from the mission God has placed before him.

Similarly, in Numbers 13:30, Caleb faces a crowd filled with fear after spying out the Promised Land. While others focus on the giants in the land, Caleb quiets the people and declares, *"We should go up and take possession of the land, for we certainly can do it."* Caleb's confidence wasn't in his own strength but in God's promise.

These moments challenge us to ask: *Whose voice are we listening to?* Like David and Caleb, we face critical voices, fearful opinions, and even doubts within ourselves. But 2 Timothy 1:7 reminds us that God has given us a spirit of power—not fear. That power, which literally means *"can,"* enables us to step into the promises God has for us, no matter the challenges ahead.

Mind Shift

1. Turn Away from the Noise: David didn't let Eliab's accusations distract him. Learn to recognize when voices—no matter how close they are—don't align with God's truth.

2. Declare God's Power: Caleb didn't deny the presence of giants, but he focused on God's ability to fulfill His promises. Let God's voice be louder than the doubts around you.

3. Walk in the Spirit of *Can*: God has given you the ability, through His Spirit, to step into His plans with faith and courage. Trust that He equips you for every battle.

4. Choose Faith Over Fear: Fearful voices will always exist, but like Caleb, you can choose to speak faith, trusting in the God who has already prepared the way.

I don't need to listen to the voices of fear, doubt, or criticism. God has given me the spirit of *can*—the power to move forward in faith and obedience.

Take a moment to reflect: Where do you need to quiet the voices around you and focus on God's truth?

Your Mind Shift

_____

_____

_____

_____

Song Suggestion

"Whom Shall I Fear (God of Angel Armies)" by Chris Tomlin

Closing Prayer

Lord, thank You for giving me a spirit of power, love, and self-discipline. Help me to quiet the voices of doubt, fear, and distraction so that I can hear You clearly. Teach me to turn away from anything that tries to pull me off course and to focus on Your promises. Strengthen my heart to walk boldly in faith, trusting in Your power and Your ability to work through me. Amen.

Devotional

Thankfulness: A Prescription for Peace

Focus Scripture

Philippians 4:6

"Do not be anxious about anything, but in every situation, by prayer and petition, with thanksgiving, present your requests to God."

Introduction

In Philippians 4:6, we are told, *"Do not be anxious about anything, but in everything, by prayer and petition, with thanksgiving, present your requests to God."* This verse speaks directly to one of the greatest struggles we face: anxiety. But hidden within this scripture is a simple yet powerful remedy that many of us tend to overlook—it's the call to bring our requests to God *with thanksgiving.*

Let's be honest—how often do we skip the thankfulness part? We come to God with our anxieties, pouring out everything we're worried about, yet it doesn't always feel like we're praying. Sometimes, it feels more like we're venting. While God is patient and loving enough to listen to us no matter how we approach Him, this pattern often leaves us feeling more overwhelmed. Why? Because we're missing a key part of the equation: gratitude.

Core Message

Think of Philippians 4:6 as a divine prescription for peace. But what happens if we don't follow the directions? If we reverse the process, it reads more like a prescription for anxiety: worry about everything, pray about nothing, and be ungrateful. This guarantees one thing—no peace.

When the Bible urges us to pray with thanksgiving, it's not a suggestion. It's an invitation to a transformative way of thinking and living. Thanksgiving shifts our focus. Instead of fixating on what's wrong or what we lack, gratitude reminds us of God's faithfulness and provision. It stirs up memories of all the times He has shown up for us. It builds our faith by pointing us back to His goodness.

Gratitude Changes Everything

Have you ever noticed how being thankful can change your perspective? Gratitude is more than just an attitude; it's a habit. And like any habit, it takes practice. Thankfulness is something I intentionally build into my daily life. Every morning, I start my prayer by simply telling God, "Thank You." I thank Him for waking me up, for my family, for His provision. Even when I'm struggling, I look for reasons to be grateful.

I've also passed this habit on to my kids. Whenever they're in a bad mood or complaining, I ask them to tell me three things they're thankful for. It's become a routine, and yes, I always throw in a little humor. "Don't forget to be thankful that you have a hot mom," I tell them, and they laugh. But the laughter breaks the tension, and suddenly, their mood begins to shift. Gratitude really does change our outlook on life.

Gratitude as a Weapon Against Anxiety

When we're overwhelmed by anxiety, gratitude feels counterintuitive. Our minds want to focus on the problem, replaying it over and over. But when we practice gratitude, it forces us to pause and look beyond the immediate struggle. It reorients our thoughts and hearts toward God. This isn't just a spiritual principle; even psychologists have found that gratitude can improve mental health, reduce stress, and increase happiness.

So, the next time you feel anxiety creeping in, try this:

1. Stop and pray. Bring your request to God. Don't hold back— tell Him what's on your heart.

2. Be intentional about thanksgiving. In the same way that you feel the emotions of your concerns and worries, relive the moments your thankful for. Thank Him for what He's already done. Recall specific moments of His faithfulness. Squeeze some more goodness out of His past provisions.

3. Make it a habit. Gratitude is like a muscle; the more you use it, the stronger it gets. Start small, and build from there.

Mind Shift

Developing a habit of gratitude doesn't mean life will always be easy, but it does mean you'll have a different perspective. Here are a few ways to make thankfulness a daily practice:

- Morning Gratitude: Start your day by listing three things you're thankful for. They don't have to be big—sometimes the small things, like a good cup of coffee or a beautiful sunrise, are enough to spark joy.

- Gratitude Journal: Write down moments of thankfulness throughout your day. It can be a brief note, but over time, you'll have a tangible record of God's faithfulness.

- Thankfulness in Prayer: Make thanksgiving a consistent part of your prayer life. Before you ask for anything, spend time thanking God for who He is and what He has done.

- Teach Gratitude: If you have kids, involve them in this practice. Challenge them to find things to be thankful for, even in tough situations. It's a life skill that will serve them well.

Ultimately, thankfulness is about more than words; it's about the posture of our hearts. It's choosing to trust God, even when we don't see the full picture. It's remembering that He is in control and that His plans for us are good. When we approach Him with thanksgiving, it draws us closer to His peace—a peace that goes beyond understanding, guarding our hearts and minds in Christ Jesus.

Let's make thankfulness a daily practice, not just an occasional act. Because when we live with a heart of gratitude, it changes everything. It's not just a path to peace—it's a way to experience the fullness of life in God.

Your Mind Shift

_____

_____

_____

_____

Song Suggestion

Never Lost by CeCe Winans

Closing Prayer

God please give me eyes to see Your Hand in all the little things around me. I want to have a thankful heart today and every day. You have been faithful to me in so many way, ways that I"m sure I have overlooked. The hard things seems so big. Change my view to see You all around me, to remember the ways You have shown up before. I know You are at work in all the places of my life. And just saying that makes me smile right now. Please teach me to lean into and practice gratitude and never take your love and faithfulness for granted. I can do this through Your strength in me. In Jesus name. Amen.

Devotional

God Never Tires of Encouraging Us

Focus Scripture

Joshua 1:9

Have I not commanded you? Be strong and courageous. Do not be afraid; do not be discouraged, for the LORD your God will be with you wherever you go."

Introduction

One of the most beautiful truths about God is that He never grows weary of encouraging us. His love is steady, and His desire to lift us up is constant, no matter how many times we may need it.

This truth became incredibly real to me one morning when I woke up feeling completely defeated. My thoughts were clouded with negativity, and I found myself frustrated. *I have walked with the Lord for 33 years—so why was I still battling discouragement?*

Why did I still need to fight to realign my mind with God's truth? Surely, I should have "arrived" by now.

Core Message

As I wrestled with my thoughts, the Holy Spirit gently prompted me to open my Bible to Joshua chapter one. There, God reminded me of an important lesson: even the most courageous and faithful leaders need encouragement. Four times in that chapter, God told Joshua to *be strong and courageous.* Four times, He reminded Joshua *not to be afraid or discouraged,* reassuring him that He would be with him wherever he went.

This reminder hit me like a wave of grace. Joshua wasn't just any leader. Forty years earlier, he was one of the two spies who had believed God could lead the Israelites into the Promised Land when the rest of the people doubted. He had faith when others didn't. Yet here he was, on the verge of leading the nation into their inheritance, needing God to encourage him again and again.

God didn't look at Joshua and say, *"How are you still afraid after all this time?"* He didn't get frustrated or impatient. Instead, He reminded him of the truth, giving him the courage he needed to move forward.

That morning, God reminded me of this same truth: He doesn't tire of encouraging us, no matter how often we need it.

A Daily Choice

That morning, I made a decision. If I needed to pray and refocus my heart every single day for the rest of my life, I would do it. I would take off fear, anxiety, doubt, and the fear of people's opinions. I would take off the fear of being abandoned or rejected. If I needed to lay those burdens down every day and put on humility, compassion, and the mind of Christ, then so be it.

This wasn't a decision born out of frustration or self-pity—it was a choice to do what was necessary to walk in step with the Holy Spirit. If that's what it takes to live in freedom, then it's worth it. I remember a song by my friend Tori G that says, *"I decided to do something different."* That's what I had to do—I had to change how I saw these moments of discouragement. Instead of seeing them as a sign of weakness, I began to see them as an opportunity to use the tools God had given me to grow stronger.

God has given us everything we need to overcome the lies and burdens of this world. He invites us to take off the old patterns and habits that weigh us down and put on His truth. But it's a daily choice. Just as Joshua needed to be reminded to be strong and courageous, we need to remind ourselves of God's promises and lean on Him every day.

Turning Toward God

God doesn't get tired of us turning to Him. He is always there, ready to lift our heads and remind us of who He is and who we are in Him. The problem isn't that we need encouragement—it's when we try to handle life on our own without turning to God for help. When we listen to the voice of fear or doubt instead of His Spirit, we miss out on the peace and strength He longs to give us.

God is waiting for us to listen to Him—to listen to His Word and believe what He says. Just as He encouraged Joshua, He wants to encourage you. He wants to remind you to be strong and courageous, to not be afraid, and to trust that He is with you wherever you go.

Mind Shift

If you're feeling discouraged today, remember that God doesn't see you as weak because you need His help. He sees you as His beloved child, and He is more than willing to remind you of His truth again and again. You're not a failure because you need encouragement. You're human, and God's grace is more than enough for you.

Your Mind Shift

_____

_____

_____

_____

Song Suggestion

"Set Me Free" by Tori G

Closing Prayer

Lord, thank You for never growing tired of encouraging me. Thank You for reminding me of Your promises and for being with me, even when I feel weak or discouraged. Help me to take off fear, doubt, and anxiety, and to put on the mind of Christ every single day. Give me the courage to trust You and to walk in step with Your Spirit. Thank You for Your patience and love. I choose to turn to You today and every day. Amen.

God doesn't tire of encouraging us. He is faithful to meet us right where we are and to give us exactly what we need to take the next step. All we have to do is turn to Him and trust that He is with us, just as He was with Joshua. So be strong and courageous, not because you never feel [Pafraid, but because God is with you wherever you go.

Devotional

Rooted Like a Dandelion

Focus Scripture

Ephesians 3:17-18

So that Christ may dwell in your hearts through faith. And I pray that you, being rooted and established in love, 18 may have power, together with all the Lord's holy people, to grasp how wide and long and high and deep is the love of Christ

---

Introduction

Dandelions are fascinating little flowers. Many see them as nothing more than weeds, something to get rid of, but their resilience is inspiring. Their roots can grow up to three feet deep, anchoring them firmly in the ground. No matter how many times you try to pull them up or how much weed killer you pour on them, they just keep popping back up. They keep growing. They keep shining with that bright yellow color, refusing to give up.

I can't help but think, *What if I could be like a dandelion?* What if I could be so deeply rooted in Christ's love that no matter what came my way—whether it was life's challenges, other people's opinions, or even my own doubts—I would still shine and grow?

Core Message

In Ephesians 3:17, Paul encourages us to be rooted and established in Christ's love. He goes on to describe how deep, wide, long, and high that love is. It's a love that can't be measured, a love that strengthens us and fills us in ways nothing else can. When we're rooted in His love, it doesn't matter how many storms we face. We'll keep standing, and we'll keep growing, just like that dandelion.

The secret to the dandelion's resilience is its roots. Those deep roots allow it to draw the nutrients and strength it needs to thrive, even in tough conditions. That's exactly what God's love does for us when we stay rooted in Him. His love becomes our source—our confidence, strength, and guide.

So often, we can get caught up in trying to please people or seeking approval from the world. We try to find our confidence in how others see us or in our accomplishments. But none of that will ever fill us the way God's love does. Ephesians 3:20 reminds us that, through His power, we can do immeasurably more than all we could ask or imagine through His power within us. That's the kind of life we're called to live—one where God's strength works in us to accomplish things far beyond what we think is possible.

But it starts with being rooted.

Staying rooted in Christ's love also means making Him the audience we live for. It's so easy to let the opinions of others influence us, but when we live to please God, our focus shifts. We stop worrying about what people think, and instead, we start living with boldness and confidence.

The dandelion doesn't worry about whether people see it as a flower or a weed. It just grows. It just shines. That's the kind of confidence we can have when we're deeply rooted in God's love. We know who we are, and we know whose we are.

Mind Shift

If you're feeling unsure of yourself or struggling to stay strong in your faith, take a moment to think about the dandelion. Let it remind you of what it looks like to be deeply rooted, to keep growing and shining no matter what. Dandelions also close up when it rains and in the evenings to keep the dew out. The very water they need to survive can take their pollen away if they soak it up from the top. Pollen gives the dandelion strength and the ability to reproduce. If the dandelion wants to use that life-giving water, it must not receive it from the top but soak it in through its roots. All of the love, support and praise that we receive must be taken in through our roots. It causes us to receive it all as a gift but not as our Source. We are dependent on our roots in Christ and He gets us everything that we need. Sometimes that comes from the outside world in praise and love. And that is wonderful. It is not our Source though. If it becomes our Source, then we are a slave to it. We must continue to work for the praise and love. In the same way that the rain can take away the dandelions strength and ability to reproduce, 'peoples love and affirmation can take ours too. It is a beautiful thing, helpful and necessary just like the rain and dew, when it is received as a gift from Christ through our roots and not as our Source itself. And when the enemy attacks (weed killer) we must receive it through the roots of Christs love which won't allow the lie of the enemy to poison us.

Ask yourself: Where are my roots? Am I drawing my strength from God's love, or am I trying to find it somewhere else? Am I letting the praise and love from others become my Source, instead of receiving their love from You? Is there anything in my life that I am receiving from the top instead of through my roots, making it my Source?

The beautiful thing is that God's love is always there. All we have to do is choose to root ourselves in Him and allow His love to fill and strengthen us.

Let's aim to be like that dandelion. Let's stay deeply rooted in Christ's love, growing and shining, no matter what comes our way.

Your Own Mind Shift

_____

_____

_____

_____

Song Suggestion

That's How Much I Love You by Kathy Troccoli

Closing Prayer

Lord, thank You for Your deep and unchanging love. Help me to stay rooted in You, to draw my strength from Your love, and to live with confidence, knowing that You are my source. When life gets tough, remind me to turn to You and to trust that Your love is enough to sustain me. May I shine with Your light and keep growing, just like the dandelion. Amen.

Be rooted. Be resilient. And remember, God's love is the foundation that will never fail you.

Devotional

Learning to Stay Free After Becoming Free

Focus Scripture

Proverbs 4:25-26

Let your eyes look straight ahead; fix your gaze directly before you. Give careful thought to the paths for your feet and be steadfast in all your ways.

Introduction

Freedom is a beautiful thing, but staying free? That's where the real work begins. I want to share a piece of my journey with you— not because I have it all figured out, but because I need the reminder too. Teaching something often cements it deeper in my own heart.

Picking up old baggage is surprisingly easy. It's like slipping on a worn-out pair of shoes—familiar, even comfortable. These bags can show up in relationships, in how we react to certain situations, and even in the quiet of our own thoughts. My path to living free has been full of ups and downs, and I've learned that the process itself is part of God's design.

Core Message

Proverbs 4:25-26 says, *"Let your eyes look straight ahead; fix your gaze directly before you. Give careful thought to the paths for your feet and be steadfast in all your ways."* These verses resonate deeply with me, especially as I reflect on my old journals. Revisiting those pages wasn't about reliving the past or dwelling in regret; it was about allowing the Holy Spirit to remind me of lessons He had already taught me—lessons I needed to relearn. Sometimes, renewing our minds means revisiting truths we've known before to keep old thought patterns from creeping back in.

One thing I've realized is that freedom isn't just about breaking chains; it's about not picking them back up after they're broken. For me, freedom hinges on two major lessons:

1. Letting go of other people's expectations and opinions to embrace the person God created me to be.

2. Forgiving myself for the ways I've fallen short.

Both have been huge, transformative steps.

Letting Go of Expectations

A quote I read once said, "Forgiveness is giving up on a better past." That was so clear for me. It reminded me of a day I had written about in my journal. I was preparing to leave for my Uncle Fred's funeral and found myself stressing about what to wear. My mind spiraled into worries about what people might think—even imagining what my dad might say. But in that moment, God's truth broke through, and I said out loud, *"I will be exactly me today. Nothing more, nothing less."* And with that came peace—beautiful, mature peace.

Transforming my mind to embrace who I am has been a journey. There was a time when I felt like I needed to prove that I was okay, that I was strong. I even had an anthem—my "Fight Song"—to push me forward. But now, even though my life is far from perfect, I've started to let go of the need to prove anything. Some days, I can just *be*, and it's amazing.

Forgiving Myself

The day after that moment of peace, I found myself in a dark place again, wrestling with guilt. I wrote about how God had forgiven me—for not being a better wife, for investing so much in ministry that I neglected my home, and for the ways I had hurt my biological children while trying to save my adopted daughter.

Facing the real me and choosing to forgive myself was one of the hardest things I've ever done.

But in forgiving myself, I discovered a deeper freedom. Other people's opinions didn't carry the same weight anymore. I had compassion for others in ways I hadn't before because I could see their journeys as separate from mine. God was teaching me to fix my eyes on the path ahead and to trust Him with the road behind me. And as I embraced His forgiveness and love, I could blaze a path of freedom for others watching my journey.

Mind Shift

I'm still learning, but here are some things that have helped me stay free:

1. Ask God to reveal your part.

When I was going through my divorce, my ex-husband's unfaithfulness was obvious. But I knew I had a part to own too. I prayed and asked God to show me my role in the situation. It took time, but He gently uncovered it. I had covered my mistakes with good intentions, but those intentions didn't erase the pain I had caused.

Facing my own faults wasn't easy, but it was necessary. It disarmed the enemy. When accusations came—whether from others or my own mind—I could stand firm and say, "Yes, I did that. I've owned it. I've asked for forgiveness, and it has no power over me anymore."

2. Embrace your strengths.

God has given me some amazing gifts, and I'm learning to live them out without fear or apology. It's not about arrogance; it's about stewardship—using what He's placed in me for His glory.

3. Keep learning in your weak areas.

I'm not perfect, and I'm okay with that. I have a counselor who helps me work through things. I regularly renew my mind with God's Word. Old baggage can be tempting to pick back up, but staying free means being intentional about putting it down every day.

Living free isn't a one-time decision; it's a daily commitment. There are moments when old patterns try to resurface, but God is faithful. He reminds me to fix my eyes on the path ahead and to trust Him with the process. Freedom isn't about perfection—it's about progress. It's about living in the truth that we are loved, forgiven, and free—not just for a moment, but for a lifetime.

What is God wanting to shift in your mind—not only to set you free, but to ensure that you stay free? Do you need to seek out a counselor or take ownership of your past? Maybe you need to forgive yourself?

Your Mind Shift

_____

_____

_____

_____

_____

_____

Song Suggestion

New by Lauren Daigle

Closing Prayer

Lord it says in Your Word that anyone who Jesus sets free is free indeed. I want that! Please search my heart and show me anything that I need to take responsibility for. Help me to forgive myself and make amends where I can. I am learning to live free. I do not want to pick up old patterns. I am new. I believe this Truth today.

Anchor it deep in me. I am Yours, chosen, forgiven, new! In Jesus name, amen.

Day 20

Growing Your Roots

CONGRATS! You have been intentionally spending time with God and His Word for 20 days. If you are like me you may have started and stopped this devotional a few times. If you have not missed one day, great. If you have missed days and needed to take extra time, great. God want YOU! That is the most important part of your relationship with God, its a relationship!!

1. Quiet the Voices: 2 Timothy 1:7 "For the Spirit God gave us does not make us timid, but gives us power, love, and self-discipline."

Your Mind Shift

_____

_____

_____

_____

2. Thankfulness: A prescription for peace. Phil. 4:6 "Do not be anxious about anything, but in everything, by prayer and petition, with thanksgiving, present your requests to God."

Your Mind Shift

_____

_____

_____

_____

3. God Doesn't Tire of Encouraging You: Joshua 1:9 Have I not commanded you? Be strong and courageous. Do not be afraid; do not be discouraged, for the LORD your God will be with you wherever you go."

Your Mind Shift

_____

_____

_____

_____

4. Rooted Like a Dandelion: Ephesians 3:17-18 so that Christ may dwell in your hearts through faith. And I pray that you, being rooted and established in love, 18 may have power, together with all the Lord's holy people, to grasp how wide and long and high and deep is the love of Christ'

Your Mind Shift

_____

_____

_____

_____

5. Learning To Stay Free After Becoming Free: Proverbs 4:25-26 Let your eyes look straight ahead; fix your gaze directly before you. Give careful thought to the paths for your feet and be steadfast in all your ways.

Your Mind Shift was:

_____

_____

_____

_____

Which of these do you feel the Holy Spirit leading you to study again? Maybe one of them filled you up with God's love and you need to reread it today. Take time to do that! Your roots are growing deeper into Christ's love. Write down any new insights that you want to remember.

_____

_____

_____

_____

Closing Prayer

God, You gave us the spirit of power, of love and of a sound mind (self-control). Thank You for that. Pleae remind me that anything that comes across my mind that doesn't agree with that statement is a lie from satan. I'm so thankful for Your love and Your grace and favor in my life. Thank You for never growing tired of encouraging me. Keep growing my roots deep down into Your love so that I am full. You are my Source. Keep me steady looking to You and the next step You have me on. Please Lord renew my mind, transform my mind so that I think like You. I love You Lord. In Jesus name. Amen.

Day 21

Finishing the Week In Worship

Take time today to thank God for what He has shown you through His Word and for what He has done. Take time to thank Him for what He is going to do in and through you. If you don't have an answer for one of the prayers that is ok. Maybe this has been a rough week for you. Let God love you right where you are. Be sure to pray the prayer at the bottom though. Your heart needs to be fed His Loving Truth and Worship.

God I thank You for showing me that You are

_____

_____

_____

_____

God I thank You for what You have done

_____

_____

_____

_____

God I thank You for what I know You are doing

_____

_____

_____

_____

Go back to your favorite songs from this week and worship!!

Closing Prayer

God I am Your Child! I belong to You. I want to please You. My God and Savior keep my eyes fixed on You even when the distrations around me try and pull me away. I feel You close to me and I want to feel that more. I am so thankful that You never give up on me. You never tire of me. You are so faithful God. I commit myself to You anew. I am all Yours. In Jesus Name. Amen.

Devotional

Stay Close to the River

Focus Scripture

Psalm 1:3

"That person is like a tree planted by streams of water, which yields its fruit in season and whose leaf does not wither—whatever they do prospers."

Introduction

Have you ever noticed how quickly life can change when you're disconnected from God? It doesn't always happen suddenly. Often, it's a slow drift—a missed prayer here, a neglected Bible reading there. Before long, what once felt vibrant and full of life starts to feel distant and dry.

Psalm 1 gives us a beautiful image of what it means to stay connected to God. It describes a person who delights in His Word as *a tree planted by streams of water,* constantly nourished and fruitful.

Rodney, Mississippi, tells a different story. Once a thriving town along the Mississippi River, it was nearly chosen as the state capital. The river supplied everything Rodney needed: trade, growth, and life. But over time, debris and sandbars formed, separating the town from the river. Today, Rodney is a ghost town. Its decline didn't happen overnight—it was a slow fade.

Just like Rodney's separation from the river, we can slowly drift away from God when we neglect our relationship with Him. But when we stay close to the River of Life, we thrive.

Core Message

The story of Rodney, Mississippi, mirrors our spiritual lives in so many ways. When Rodney was connected to the river, it flourished. The river was its lifeline, bringing in resources, people, and vitality. But over time, as debris built up and the river shifted, the town faded. What once was alive became lifeless.

This happens when we lose connection with God, the Source of life. We might not notice it at first, but a missed prayer or a small compromise can lead to a growing distance. God blesses us with family, careers, and passions, but those blessings can become distractions if we don't remain rooted in Him.

Psalm 1 reminds us that a person planted by streams of water thrives. Their leaf does not wither, and they bear fruit in season.

Staying close to God ensures that we remain nourished, even when life gets challenging. But when we allow sin, distractions, or busyness to creep in, we risk becoming spiritually dry—just like Rodney became a ghost town.

So, how do we stay close to the River? It starts with intentionality. Make time for God. Prioritize His Word. Examine your life for anything that might be creating distance between you and Him.

Mind Shift

1. Protect Your Connection to the Source: Just as Rodney relied on the Mississippi River for life, we rely on God. Regularly examine what might be blocking your connection to Him—sin, distractions, or misplaced priorities.
2. Be Mindful of the Drift: The drift away from God often happens slowly. Pay attention to small compromises or missed moments with Him before they add up.
3. Stay Rooted in God's Word: The person described in Psalm 1 delights in God's Word and meditates on it day and night. This daily nourishment keeps us spiritually strong.
4. Don't Let Blessings Replace the Giver: The blessings God gives us are wonderful, but they are not the Source. Stay focused on God, who provides all you need.

I will protect my connection to God, the Source of life, and stay rooted in Him. His presence is what sustains me, not the blessings He provides.

Take a moment to reflect: What is creating distance between you and God? How can you stay close to the River of Life? Write your mind shift thought here:

Your Mind Shift

_____

_____

_____

_____

Song Suggestion

Slow Fade by Casting Crowns

Closing Prayer

Lord, thank You for being my River of Life. Help me to stay connected to You in every season. Show me anything that is creating distance between us, and help me remove it. I don't want to drift away, Lord. Keep me rooted in Your Word and faithful to Your call. Thank You for sustaining me and for the blessings You pour into my life. In Jesus' name, Amen.

Devotional

Selling the Business

Focus Scripture

Psalm 21:2

"You have granted him his heart's desire and have not withheld the request of his lips."

Introduction

Sometimes, the desires of our hearts take years to be fulfilled. During that waiting season, God grows our faith and teaches us to trust Him in ways we never imagined. But even when He answers those prayers, we can still feel a mix of joy and uncertainty. I remember the time I sold my business, and it was one of those moments where God fulfilled a long-held desire of my heart. Yet, the process wasn't without challenges or unexpected reminders of His presence.

Selling the business was something I had prayed for over two years. By the time the opportunity came, I had a six-month-old baby and was ready to focus fully on being a stay-at-home mom. Even though I knew this was God's plan, I found myself anxious the night before signing the papers. That night, God met me in His Word, reassuring my heart that He was in control.

Core Message

The years leading up to selling the business were full of faith-stretching moments. Financial struggles, impossible schedules, and endless "what-ifs" became part of my daily life. Yet, God repeatedly showed up. One story still stands out to me:

I had sent out payroll checks, but there wasn't enough money in the account to cover them. I prayed and trusted that, as He had done so many times before, God would provide. Friday arrived, and I confidently went to the mailbox, expecting the usual customer check that would solve everything. But this time, there was no check. I remember asking God, "Am I really going to have to call my employee and tell her the check isn't good?"

Then, God showed His sense of humor. I got a call from a dentist's office in Auburn Hills, an hour away. Somehow, one of our payroll checks had been delivered there. Everything on the envelope was correct, but God had clearly messed with the mail! I had to explain to my employee that her check would be late, but the very next day, a customer's check arrived—just in time to cover payroll.

This was the kind of faith God had been growing in me: learning to trust Him in the unexpected and the impossible. That trust was about to be tested again as I prepared to sell the business.

The night before signing the papers, I was nervous. The business brought in income, and even though I knew it was time to let it go, the uncertainty of what came next weighed on me. I opened my Bible to Psalm 21, following my habit of reading the Psalm for the day. When I read, "You have granted him his heart's desire and have not withheld the request of his lips," I felt peace wash over me. God was reminding me that this was His plan and that He was giving me the desires of my heart.

The next day, as I drove to sign the papers, something unexpected happened. I was rear-ended at a railroad crossing with my baby, Riley, in the car. Thankfully, no one was hurt, and my car wasn't damaged, but it shook me. It was a reminder that even when we're walking in God's will, things won't always go smoothly. There will still be bumps and distractions.

Selling the business and stepping into the role of a full-time mom was one of the most beautiful times in my life. It anchored my faith and showed me that God truly does fulfill the desires of our hearts when we trust Him and wait on His timing.

Mind Shift

1. Trust God in the Waiting: Like Psalm 5:3 says, lay your requests before God and wait expectantly. Even when the answers don't come right away, He is working.

2. God's Provision is Always on Time: Whether it's payroll or peace for a big decision, God knows what we need and provides exactly when we need it.

3. Challenges Don't Mean You're Off Track: Just because you face difficulties doesn't mean you've missed God's will. Stay focused on Him, knowing He is with you every step of the way.

4. Celebrate God's Faithfulness: When He fulfills the desires of your heart, take time to recognize and celebrate His goodness. Let those moments strengthen your faith for the future.

God is faithful in every season. Even when things feel uncertain or challenging, I can trust Him to fulfill the desires of my heart in His perfect timing.

Take a moment to reflect: Where is God asking you to trust Him in the waiting? How can you celebrate His faithfulness in your life today? Write your mind shift thought here:

Your Mind Shift:

_____

_____

_____

_____

Song Suggestion

Goodness of God by Bethel Music

Closing Prayer

Lord, thank You for being a faithful and loving Father. Thank You for hearing my prayers and knowing the desires of my heart. Help me to trust You in the waiting, to recognize Your provision, and to celebrate when You fulfill Your promises. When the path feels uncertain, remind me that You are always with me. Strengthen my faith to walk in obedience and to rest in the truth of Your Word. In Jesus' name, Amen.

Devotional

Fake Fruit

Focus Scripture

John 15:3:

"I am the vine, and you are the branches. If a man remains in Me and I in him, he will bear much fruit; apart from Me you can do nothing."

Introduction

How does a branch produce fruit? It produces fruit from what it is connected to. If a branch is connected to an apple tree trunk, it will produce apples. If it is connected to a cherry tree, cherries will grow. In the same way, the fruit of the Spirit grows in us because we are connected to Jesus, the True Vine.

Fruit doesn't appear overnight; it takes time to grow. When you accepted Jesus' sacrifice for your sins, you became connected to the True Vine. Before that, you were like a broken branch on the ground—drying up and dying. But when you placed your faith in

Jesus, God the Gardener picked you up and grafted you into His family.

Core Message

Have you ever seen how grafting works? It's a slow process. The new branch doesn't immediately start bearing fruit. First, it must adjust, grow, and receive nutrients from the vine. When we come to Jesus, the same thing happens. Our transformation is gradual. As we remain connected to Him, the fruit of the Spirit—*love, joy, peace, patience, kindness, goodness, faithfulness, gentleness, and self-control*—begins to grow in our lives.

But here's an important truth: fake fruit isn't necessary.

Beware of Fake Fruit

Sometimes, we feel pressured to dress ourselves up to look like we're growing faster than we are. Maybe it's to fit in with a church family, or perhaps we feel the need to appear as if we have everything together. But when we put on fake fruit, it only hides what's truly happening in our hearts.

Church family, let's not encourage our brothers and sisters to focus on outward behaviors. The goal isn't to *look* the part but to *stay connected* to the True Vine. This connection is where real growth happens.

For those who are newly grafted into God's family, take a deep breath. You don't have to rush or pretend. Enjoy getting to know Jesus. Spend time in His presence, learning to abide in Him. Real fruit will come—but it takes time.

Plastic Fruit Can Kill

Have you ever tried to eat a piece of plastic fruit? It looks good from the outside, but it's empty and useless. If someone tried to bite into it, they'd quickly regret it. Fake fruit in our spiritual lives works the same way. When we focus on appearances instead of abiding in Jesus, we not only stunt our own growth but might also hurt others who look to us for encouragement or guidance.

For those who've been walking with the Lord for some time, ask yourself: *Are you still tending to your connection with Jesus?* Abiding isn't a one-time action—it's a lifelong commitment to stay rooted in Him. When you nurture that connection, His life flows through you, producing fruit that nourishes others.

Mind Shift

1. Are you trying to produce fruit in your own strength? Write down ways you've been striving instead of abiding.

2. How can you spend intentional time this week staying connected to Jesus?

3. Reflect on any "fake fruit" you've relied on in the past. Ask Jesus to replace it with real, life-giving fruit.

Your Mind Shift

_____

_____

_____

_____

_____

_____

Song Suggestion

"I Give You My Heart" by Hillsong

Let this song remind you of the beauty of staying connected to Jesus, the True Vine. Listen, worship, and let the words minister to your heart as you spend time in His presence.

Closing Prayer

Lord Jesus, thank You for reminding me that my connection to You is the most important part of my walk. Teach me to abide in You, to rest in Your presence, and to allow Your Spirit to grow real fruit in my life. Help me to let go of appearances and fake fruit and instead focus on staying rooted in You. Thank You for being patient with me as I grow. I surrender myself to You again today. In Your name, Amen.

Devotional

Just Do It

Focus Scripture

---

2 Kings 5

In 2 Kings 5:11, Naaman says, "I thought that he would surely come out to me and stand and call on the name of the Lord his God, wave his hand over the spot, and cure me of my leprosy."

Introduction

That verse fascinates me.

Naaman was a man of success—a valiant leader, powerful, and respected. Yet all his accomplishments didn't erase his need. I imagine he tried to avoid thinking about his leprosy, convincing himself he could manage it. But when the servant girl mentioned a cure, something inside him stirred, and he took a risk by acting on her advice.

It wasn't easy for him to admit he needed help. He had to go to the king and ask for a letter. He had to expose his weakness. Vulnerability is hard, isn't it? Especially when you're in a position of strength or authority.

Core Message

Naaman traveled with hope in his heart. The Word tells us that Naaman had a very clear expectation of how this healing was going to go. He was use to being in charge. However, Elisha didn't get Naaman's memo. Elisha sent a messenger to tell Naaman to wash in the Jordan River seven times. That was it.

Naaman was angry. This wasn't what he imagined at all. Here he was, in a foreign land, being asked to do something so ordinary, so beneath him. He was ready to walk away and give up.

How often do we do the same? When God's answer to our prayers doesn't match the picture in our heads, we hesitate. We resist. Sometimes, we'd rather give up than follow through with something that feels too simple, too ordinary, or just not what we expected.

Thankfully, Naaman wasn't alone. His servants saw his frustration and spoke up. They didn't mock him or scold him. Instead, they reasoned with him, gently but firmly. "If the prophet had told you to do something great, wouldn't you have done it? How much more, then, when he tells you to wash and be cleansed?"

We all need people like that in our lives—truth-tellers who encourage us to see past our pride and keep going when obedience feels hard.

Naaman listened. He went down to the Jordan, dipped himself seven times, and was healed. His skin was restored, but something even greater happened. He encountered the God of Israel and knew, without a doubt, that there was no other God.

This wasn't just physical healing for Naaman; it was spiritual transformation. He asked for soil from Israel, wanting to take a piece of the land back home with him. He committed himself to worship only the God of Israel, even as he faced the reality of his role back home. Naaman was thoughtful about his commitment, understanding that obedience would impact every part of his life.

Obedience changes everything. It can be uncomfortable, inconvenient, or even humbling, but when we trust God enough to follow His direction, we find healing and transformation in ways we never imagined.

Mind Shift

- Are there areas in your life where you've been hesitant to obey God? What's holding you back?

- Do you surround yourself with people who will encourage you to follow through with God's instructions, even when it feels hard?

- Like Naaman, can you let go of your own picture of how God should move and simply trust Him?

Your Mind Shift

_____

_____

_____

_____

_____

_____

Song Suggestion

Build a Boat by Colton Dixon

Closing Prayer

Father, thank You for seeing past my pride and my expectations. Forgive me for the times I've resisted Your instructions because they didn't match the picture I had in my head. Help me to trust You enough to obey, even when it feels uncomfortable or small. Thank You for friends who speak truth into my life and encourage me to keep going. Teach me to recognize Your ways and follow

You wholeheartedly. I know Your plans are better than mine. Amen.

Devotional

Influence of a servant girl

Focus Scripture

---

2 Kings 5:2-3

Now bands of raiders from Aram had gone out and had taken captive a young girl from Israel, and she served Naamans's wife. She said to her mistress, "If only my master would see the prophet wo is in Samaria! He would cure him of his leprosy.

Introduction

In our last devotional, we explored Naaman's story and how his obedience to God led to healing and transformation. But now, let's shift our focus to a quieter figure in the same chapter—the servant girl.

Core Message

In 2 Kings 5:2, we learn that this young girl was taken captive from Israel and brought to serve in Naaman's household. Imagine her life: she was ripped away from her family, her home, and her culture, placed in a foreign land, and forced to live as a servant. This wasn't her dream. It wasn't her plan. But even in this place of pain and displacement, she continued to live out her faith in God.

When she said to her mistress, "If only my master would see the prophet who is in Samaria! He would cure him of his leprosy" (verse 3), her words carried weight. Somehow, this servant girl had lived in such a way that her words were taken seriously—even by a commander like Naaman, who held a position of great authority.

She could have chosen bitterness. She could have stayed silent, angry at her circumstances. But instead, she chose faithfulness. Her simple statement set in motion a chain of events that not only healed Naaman but also changed his heart and the community around him.

Lessons from the Servant Girl

1. Stay faithful

2. The servant girl was in a place she didn't want to be, yet she stayed faithful to God. Her story reminds us that even when life doesn't look the way we hoped, God can still use us. We don't have to understand how He's working. We just have to stay connected to Him and trust that He's moving in ways we can't see.

3. Do the simple things.

4. God often asks us to do small, seemingly insignificant things, like the servant girl speaking up or Naaman washing in the Jordan. These acts may not look dramatic, but they carry the potential for incredible impact. The servant girl's willingness to speak was the catalyst for a miracle.

5. Trust God's methods.

6. God doesn't always answer our prayers or solve our problems the way we think He should. His ways are higher than ours. Personally, I've seen this in my life. My divorce was painful, but God used it to teach me how to love myself. He slowed me down, helped me own my mistakes, and reminded me that His love is unshakable.

I didn't need to figure out how God was going to use that season of my life for good. I just needed to stay connected to Him, to trust that He had a plan, and to take one step at a time.

Mind Shift

- Where in your life do you feel displaced or out of place, like the servant girl? How can you trust that God is using you there?

- What simple act of obedience is God asking you to take right now?

- Are you willing to surrender your picture of how life should look and trust God's better plan?

Your Mind Shift

_____

_____

_____

_____

_____

_____

Song Suggestion

He's Been Faithful by Taranda Greene with Brooklyn Tabernacle Choir

Closing Prayer

Lord, You are faithful even in the places I don't want to be. Thank You for reminding me through this servant girl that You can use me in ways I may never fully understand. Help me to stay connected to You, to trust Your methods, and to do the simple things You ask of me. I surrender my plans, my expectations, and my picture of how life should look. Use me in the ways You see fit, and let my life point others to You. In Jesus name, Amen.

Day 27

Growing Your Roots

Remember that today is the most important day of this devotional. Today you will look back, like you have been, at the mind shifts the Holy Spirit is opening your eyes to. Today you intentionally take time to feed those Truths of Gods Word so that they are more than a momentary peace, but a peace everlasting.

1. Stay Close To The River: Psalm 1:3 "That person is like a tree planted by streams of water, which yields its fruit in season and whose leaf does not wither—whatever they do prospers."

Your Mind Shift

_____

_____

_____

_____

_____

2. Selling The Business: Psalm 21:2 "You have granted him his heart's desire and have not withheld the request of his lips."

Your Mind Shift

_____

_____

_____

_____

_____

_____

3. Fake Fruit: John 15:3: "I am the vine, and you are the branches. If a man remains in Me and I in him, he will bear much fruit; apart from Me you can do nothing."

Your Mind Shift

_____

_____

_____

_____

_____

_____

4. Just Do It: 2 Kings 5:11, Naaman says, "I thought that he would surely come out to me and stand and call on the name of the Lord his God, wave his hand over the spot, and cure me of my leprosy."

Your Mind Shift

_____

_____

_____

_____

_____

_____

5. Influence of a Servant Girl: 2 Kings 5:2-3 Now bands of raiders from Aram had gone out and had taken captive a young girl from Israel, and she served Naamans's wife. She said to her mistress, "If only my master would see the prophet wo is in Samaria! He would cure him of his leprosy.

Your Mind Shift

_____

_____

_____

_____

_____

_____

What is the Holy Spirit prompting you to focus on today? Go back and reread that devotional. Write down any new insights or mind shifts that God shows you.

_____

_____

_____

_____

_____

Closing Prayer

Lord my desire is to keep close to You. I ask You to search me to see if there is anything seperating us. Thank You for blessing me with the desires of my heart, but my first desire is to stay close to You. As I abide and grow in my connection with You, I know that You will grow fruit from my life. Please show me any area that I have been decorating myself with fake fruit. Oh Lord may I do what You ask and the way You ask, not thinking that it has to go my way. You are not a pharmacist that I give my own prescription to and expect You to fill it. I am Your servant. And may I live fully in the place that You have me today, knowing that You will use my life for Your Glory right here. In Jesus name. Amen.

Day 28

Finishing the Week In Worship

Today, look back at your entries from Days 6, 13, and 20, and ask the Holy Spirit to reveal a specific truth that needs to be nurtured in your life. He knows exactly what is ahead and what you need.

Don't rush today. Listen and obey.

Lord, show me the feast in Your Word that I need right now. Show me where to dig in. And, Lord, grow my roots deeper in You.

In Jesus' Name, Amen.

Write down any new insights or mindset shifts that you need to remember below:

:_____

_____

_____

_____

_____

_____

Devotional

Free from Comparison

Focus Scripture

Galatians 6:4

*"Each one should test their own actions. Then
they can take pride in themselves alone,
without comparing themselves to someone else,
for each one should carry their own load."*

Introduction

In my 20s, I was a young mom trying to prove that I was enough. The need to measure up seemed to follow me everywhere. I wanted to be a good mom so badly that I constantly found myself comparing my parenting to other mothers.

One day, I took my six-month-old daughter, Taylor, to a swim class. The instructor handed us life jackets and told us to practice pulling our babies to safety. Taylor loved the water, so this task was easy for me. As I swam across the pool with her floating peacefully behind me, she was so relaxed that she fell asleep! I felt proud and wanted someone to notice how *"perfectly"* I had handled the exercise.

But right then, the Holy Spirit whispered, *"This isn't a competition."*

That moment opened my eyes. God began showing me all the ways I was comparing myself to others—whether it was how long I nursed Taylor, her nap schedule, or our bedtime routine. It was as if He was replaying clips of my life, revealing how desperately I was trying to prove I was a good mom.

Core Message

God led me to Galatians 6:4, which reminded me that my actions should be tested on their own merit, not against someone else's. Then He showed me John 3:17: *"For God did not send His Son into the world to condemn the world, but to save the world through Him."*

God wasn't condemning me; He was shining light on the sin of comparison to save me from it.

He began to highlight the unique ways women around me parented. One of my friends thrived on keeping her five kids busy with activities—they were at a game or practice almost every day. Meanwhile, my kids stayed home, built forts, played in the mud, and rode their bikes. Both of us were good moms. We just parented differently.

Some of my friends were passionate about recycling and eating organic. I admired their efforts, but it wasn't my priority. God was teaching me that I didn't need to be just like them. He was unlocking the jail cell of comparison and showing me how to celebrate the uniqueness He gave me—and my friends.

Lessons in Uniqueness

Over time, I learned that loving myself freed me to love others better. My friends being good moms didn't make me less of one, and me being a good mom didn't diminish their efforts.

Even now, with grown children, comparison tries to creep in. I sometimes see my past mistakes or fear I'm messing up again without realizing it. God gently reminds me to trust Him, to keep learning, and to give myself grace.

He also reminds me of a truth I hold close: God gave my children the mom they needed—me.

Finding Your Freedom

Freedom from comparison doesn't come all at once, but as we grow in our faith, God teaches us to embrace who He created us to be. One of my favorite quotes from the movie *Dumplin'* says it perfectly: *"Find out who you are and do it on purpose."*

We're all made to reflect God's image in a unique way. Think about it—apple trees don't try to become pine trees. They simply produce apples because that's what they're meant to do. If we could accept that same truth for ourselves, we'd have so much more peace.

Comparison steals joy not just in parenting but in every area of life—our marriages, careers, bodies, personalities, and more. Learning to like who God made us to be is a lifelong process, but it's also a beautiful one.

Mind Shift

- Where are you struggling with comparison? How has it been stealing your joy?

- Reflect on how God has made you unique. Are there ways He's calling you to celebrate that?

- Who in your life could you cheer on today, knowing their success doesn't diminish your own?

Your Mind Shift

_____

_____

_____

_____

_____

Song Suggestion

"Who You Say I Am" by Hillsong Worship – A powerful reminder of who we are in Christ.

Closing Prayer

Lord, thank You for making me unique. Forgive me for comparing myself to others and forgetting that You've created me with purpose. Help me to see myself through Your eyes and to celebrate the person You've made me to be. Teach me to love others without falling into the trap of comparison. Thank You for setting me free and reminding me that I am enough because of You. In Jesus Name, Amen.

Flying, Falling, and Catching: Trusting God in Every Leap

Focus Scripture

Deuteronomy 20:4

"For the Lord your God is the one who goes with you to fight for you against your enemies to give you victory."

Introduction

Have you ever watched a trapeze artist fly through the air? It's captivating—the way they swing, twist, and let go, trusting their partner to catch them midair. Henry Nouwen saw something profoundly spiritual in the way trapeze artists lived out trust, risk, and surrender. He intended to write a book about it, but his friend finished the work for him after his passing. The imagery stuck with me too, as I've reflected on my own journey with God.

Core Message

The Lord has asked me to take some courageous leaps in my life. Sometimes, they've been exhilarating—like when I took a bold step of faith in ministry. I nodded "yes" to God's prompting, and He opened doors I never imagined. It felt like flying, soaring through the air, and landing perfectly in the catcher's hands. But not all my leaps have gone so smoothly. Some have left me feeling like I jumped into thin air with no one there to catch me.

The hardest leaps for me have been in love. I've been married and divorced twice, and my second marriage left deep scars. At the time, I couldn't see the emotional and spiritual abuse for what it was. I kept trying to fix things, kept trying to hold on, believing it was my responsibility to make it work. It wasn't until God opened my eyes that I could see clearly and understand I needed to let go. Walking away was one of the hardest things I've ever done, but it was also the beginning of my healing.

It hasn't been easy, but I've learned that even if a human partner lets me fall, my Savior never will. God has asked me over and over—in careers, in ministry, and in relationships—to be courageous. Only because of His unfailing love can I obey with boldness wherever He leads me. God has been my safety net, catching me every time I've stumbled and reminding me that His love is constant.

Whether in relationships, ministry, or other areas of life, the call to trust God is the same. Sometimes we soar, and sometimes we struggle, but God is always there. His love never fails. So, I can keep climbing the ladder and leaping, knowing that no matter what, I am secure in Him.

Scripture Reflection

"For the Lord your God is the one who goes with you to fight for you against your enemies to give you victory."

— Deuteronomy 20:4

When you feel afraid to leap, remember that God goes with you. He's fighting for you, catching you, and guiding you every step of the way.

Mind Shift

1. What area of your life feels like a trapeze leap right now?

2. How has God caught you in the past when you felt like you were falling?

3. What would change in your heart if you fully trusted God as your safety net?

Take a moment to picture yourself on that trapeze. Feel the courage it takes to let go and the peace that comes from knowing God is waiting to catch you.

Your Mind Shift

_____

_____

_____

_____

_____

_____

Song Suggestion

Listen to "Oceans (Where Feet May Fail)" by Hillsong United. Let the lyrics remind you of God's call to step out in faith and trust Him to hold you steady.

Closing Prayer

Lord, You are my safety net and my Savior. Thank You for catching me when I fall and for healing the broken places in my heart. Give me the courage to leap again, to trust You with every step, and to believe that Your love will never let me go. When I'm afraid to risk or to love, remind me that You go with me and fight for me. Help me to surrender fully to You, knowing You will always catch me.

In Jesus' name, Amen.

Devotional

A Light in the Darkness: Trusting God When You Can't See

Focus Scripture

Psalm 119:105 (MSG)

"By your words I can see where I'm going; they throw a beam of light on my dark path."

Introduction

Sometimes life feels so dark that even the next step seems impossible. That was my experience in the thick of an emotionally and spiritually abusive relationship. At the time, I couldn't see it for what it was. It blinded me, leaving me tangled in confusion and anxiety. I would pull into my own driveway, on the verge of an anxiety attack, wondering why I was so on edge. To the outside world, I looked steady, unshaken, and in control, but inside, I was crumbling.

Core Message

I kept telling myself, *"Isn't this what a good Christian does? Doesn't love mean serving and sacrificing no matter what? Shouldn't I be grateful for the little good that was left?"* I pushed myself to make things work, even when my heart knew something was deeply wrong. People around me didn't understand. They encouraged me to fix things, to keep serving, to give more of myself—even when I had nothing left to give.

The truth about emotional abuse is that it's insidious. It blinds you, making you doubt what you're feeling and question what's real. I couldn't see the unhealthy dynamics right in front of me. And as someone who's taught on boundaries and led through life-and-death situations, I struggled to accept how deeply I was ensnared. I thought I should have been stronger, more aware. But in the fog of that relationship, clarity felt out of reach.

It was on a vacation, far from the noise and expectations of daily life, that the Lord gave me a fresh understanding of Psalm 119:105. He gently whispered, *"I know you can't see right now. I know you're blinded, but trust Me. My Word is your light in the darkness. I love you, and I'm here. You don't have to figure this all out or worry about what people will think. Let Me guide you one step at a time. Let Me love you whole."*

In that moment, I realized I didn't have to have all the answers. I didn't need to explain myself or make everyone else understand. All I had to do was take the next step God showed me. He promised His Word would light my path, and He has been faithful to that promise. Day by day, He's led me out of that darkness. He's given me courage, healed my heart, and reminded me that His love is greater than any fear or shame.

This devotional isn't just about my story—it's about awareness. You may never find yourself in an emotionally or spiritually abusive relationship. If that's the case, I praise God for it. But I also want to speak to those who are or have been in similar situations. Emotional abuse doesn't leave visible bruises, but the weight of anxiety and control is real and heavy. It blinds you, isolates you, and makes you doubt who you are. It makes you feel like healing is impossible.

Many different things can entangle us and cause us to be blinded—addiction, mental health struggles, and codependency are just a few.

But hear me when I say this: *God can heal you.* His Word is a light that shines even in the darkest places. He sees what you can't, and He will guide you step by step. With Him, all things are possible.

Scripture Reflection

"By your words I can see where I'm going; they throw a beam of light on my dark path."

— Psalm 119:105 (MSG)

God's Word is more than just a guide—it's a promise. When you can't see what's ahead, His light will always show you the way.

Mind Shift

1. Are there areas of your life where you feel blinded or stuck in darkness?

2. How can you lean into God's Word for clarity and direction?

3. What step is God asking you to take today, even if you can't see the full path ahead?

Let God's Word be the light you hold tightly to as you take each step forward.

Your Mind Shift

_____

_____

_____

_____

_____

_____

Song Suggestion

Listen to "Thy Word" by Amy Grant as a reminder of God's promise to light your way, even in the darkest times.

Closing Prayer

Lord,

Thank You for being my light in the darkness. When I couldn't see, You were there, guiding me with Your Word and holding me in Your love. I ask You to continue leading me, step by step, as I heal and grow. For those who are walking through their own dark seasons, I pray You would shine Your light into their lives. Give them courage, clarity, and the assurance that You will never leave them. Remind us all that no matter how heavy life feels, Your Word is always enough to guide us through.

In Jesus' name, Amen.

Devotional

Take Your Tambourine

Focus Scriptures

Exodus 15:20

*Miriam the prophetess, Aaron's sister, took a
tambourine in her hand, and all the women
followed her, with tambourines and dancing.*

Introduction

Imagine this moment. The Israelites, who had known nothing but
slavery their entire lives, were finally free. Pharaoh, defeated and
enraged by the plagues God sent, ordered them to leave Egypt. In
the chaos and urgency, they grabbed what they could and fled.
Somehow, in the midst of all that, the women packed tambourines.

Core Message

Tambourines. Instruments of celebration. Of all the things they
could have carried into the unknown, they chose tambourines. This
simple act reveals their faith—a deep, abiding belief that there

would be a reason to rejoice. Even as they left slavery and faced the Red Sea, they believed in God's deliverance.

And God did not disappoint. When the sea split, they walked through on dry land. When the waters crashed back down, their enemies were no more. Their tambourines, which might have seemed unnecessary or out of place, became tools of worship. Miriam and the women danced, sang, and praised God with the very tambourines they had carried from Egypt.

What about us? Do we pack our tambourines? Do we carry with us the expectation of celebration even in seasons of waiting or struggle? Too often, we face challenges with dread instead of faith, forgetting how God has brought us through before. The tambourine is a reminder—of victories won, promises kept, and God's faithfulness in every trial.

Let this story challenge you to keep your tambourine close. Whatever battle, waiting period, or unknown you face, take with you the sound of praise. Remember that you serve a God who parts seas, defeats enemies, and invites you to celebrate.

Mind Shift

1. Remember Past Victories: Reflect on a time when God came through for you. Write it down as a "celebration marker" to remind yourself of His faithfulness.

2. Pack Your Tambourine: Whether literal or symbolic, choose something that reminds you to praise God even in the waiting. It could be a journal, a favorite song, or even an actual tambourine!

3. Choose Faith Over Fear: The women carried tambourines because they expected to celebrate. Pray for faith to see past your current struggles and into the joy of God's victory.

Your Mind Shift

What is your tambourine? Reflect on how God has brought you through challenges before and how you can carry that faith into your next season. Use this space to write your thoughts:

Your Mind Shift

_____

_____

_____

_____

_____

_____

Song Suggestion

"See A Victory" by Elevation Worship. Let this song remind you that God is always working for your good, and victory is assured in Him.

Closing Prayer

Dear Lord, thank You for being the God who parts seas and leads us into freedom. Help me to carry my tambourine of faith, trusting that Your deliverance will come. When I face trials, remind me of the victories You've already won in my life. Teach me to praise You in every season, knowing that You are always faithful. In Jesus' name, Amen.

Devotional

A New Way to Celebrate

Focus Scripture

Romans 2:29

No, a man is a Jew if he is one inwardly, and circumcision is circumcision of the heart, by the Spirit, not by the written law. Such a man's praise is not from men, but from God.

Introduction

Joshua 4:1–9, Joshua 5:2–9

The story of the Israelites is one of rescue, redemption, and relationship. As we reflect on their journey from Egypt to the Promised Land, we see the unmistakable hand of God at work—performing miracles and shaping His people to know Him deeply.

When God parted the Red Sea for the first generation of Israelites, their response was jubilant. They sang, danced, and celebrated their rescue with tambourines. It was a natural reaction—how could they not rejoice when God had just delivered them from 400 years of slavery? They were new to this relationship with God, still learning who He was: their Rescuer, Waymaker, Provider, and Guide.

But their faith was fragile. When they faced hardships, they doubted, complained, and rebelled. Even though they saw God's miraculous power, they lacked the trust to enter the Promised Land. Their story is a cautionary tale about faith that is tied too closely to circumstances rather than to the God behind the miracles.

Forty years later, a new generation stood at the Jordan River. Like their parents, they witnessed God part the waters so they could cross on dry ground. But their response was different. This time, the celebration wasn't just about the miracle—it was about the God who performed it.

At God's command, they built a memorial with stones taken from the river. This wasn't for decoration; it was a physical reminder of God's faithfulness. Each stone told a story, and together, they declared, *"God brought us through."* Then, in a striking act of obedience, the men were circumcised. It was a painful, personal sacrifice—a shedding of excess and a sign of their renewed commitment to God.

What a contrast. The first generation celebrated with tambourines, but the second generation celebrated by surrendering themselves.

They had grown in their faith. They weren't just focused on the miracle itself; they were focused on the Miracle Worker. Their celebration wasn't just about what God did for them but about who God was to them.

Core Message

Our walk with God is a journey. Sometimes, we're like that first generation—new to faith and just learning who God is. We rely on His daily provision, just as the Israelites depended on manna from heaven and the guidance of a cloud by day and fire by night. That's a beautiful stage—a place where we experience God's care in the most tangible ways.

But God doesn't want us to stay there. He invites us to grow. He wants to take us from a place where we celebrate the miracle to a place where we surrender to the Miracle Worker. Mature faith isn't just about circumstances changing; it's about God changing us. It's about trusting Him even when the manna stops falling and the cloud is no longer visible.

When the second generation crossed the Jordan, they weren't just walking into a new land—they were stepping into a deeper relationship with God. They weren't celebrating because the Jordan parted; they were celebrating because their hearts were aligned with God's purposes. Their faith wasn't just in the provision—it was in the Provider.

Sometimes, God's miracles call for tambourines. Other times, they call for memorial stones and circumcision. One is joyful and exuberant; the other is reflective and sacrificial. Neither is wrong, and both are part of our walk with God.

Are you in a place where you're learning to trust God for your daily needs? Rejoice in that! God is faithful to show up in ways that will grow your faith. Or are you at a point where you're ready to let go of something that's holding you back? Maybe God is calling you to surrender—to make a painful but necessary sacrifice as an act of faith.

The Israelites' journey teaches us that true celebration isn't just about what God does for us—it's about what He does in us. It's about letting His miracles transform our hearts, not just our circumstances.

Mind Shift

Take a moment to reflect:

- Are you focused on the miracle or the Miracle Worker?

- Is God asking you to celebrate with a tambourine or with a memorial stone?

- What step of faith or surrender is God inviting you to take?

Your Mind Shift

_____

_____

_____

_____

_____

Song Suggested

"More Than Anything" by Natalie Grant

Reflect on how His miracles point to His character, and let your faith grow deeper in response.

Closing Prayer

"Lord, thank You for Your miracles, both big and small. Help me to see beyond the blessing and focus on You, the One who provides. Grow my faith so that it's not tied to my circumstances but rooted in who You are. Teach me to celebrate in ways that honor You, whether that's with joy or surrender. I want to know You more deeply and trust You more fully. Amen."

Day 34

Growing Your Roots

1. Free From Comparison: Galatians 6:4 "Each one should test their own actions. Then they can take pride in themselves alone, without comparing themselves to someone else, for each one should carry their own load."

Your Mind Shift

_____

_____

_____

_____

2. Flying, Falling, Catching: Deuteronomy 20:4 "For the Lord your God is the one who goes with you to fight for you against your enemies to give you victory."

Your Mind Shift

_____

_____

_____

_____

3. Light in the Darkness; Trusting God When You Can't See: Psalm 119:105 (MSG) "By your words I can see where I'm going; they throw a beam of light on my dark path."

Your Mind Shift

_____

_____

_____

_____

4. Take Your Tambourine: Exodus 15:20 *Miriam the prophetess, Aaron's sister, took a tambourine in her hand, and all the women followed her, with tambourines and dancing. —* Exodus 15:20

Your Mind Shift

_____

_____

_____

_____

5. A New Way to Celebrate: Romans 2:29 No, a man is a Jew if he is one inwardly, and circumcision is circumcision of the heart, by the Spirit, not by the written, Such a man's praise is not from men, but from God. Joshua 4:1–9, Joshua 5:2–9

Your Mind Shift

_____

_____

_____

_____

What is the focused devotional that you feel the Holy Spirit is asking you to dive into a little bit more? Take time to reread that devotional again today, and feed that seed that has been planted in your heart. Write any new insights that you need to remember, below.

_____

_____

_____

_____

Closing Prayer

Lord God, I thank You for making me exactly the way You did. I am a masterpiece—Your handiwork. Help me to enjoy the *me* that You created without comparing myself to someone else. Give me the courage to fly, knowing that Your love is my net. I am never alone or without my Savior.

Thank You for shining light on my path with Your Word so that I can navigate this life. My tambourine is in my hand. I am looking expectantly at my future, ready to celebrate all the moments—big and small. But take me even deeper than that. Bring me to the place where I celebrate not only with a tambourine but with the full surrender of my heart.

In Jesus' Name, Amen.

Day 35

Finishing the Week In Worship

What a journey we are on with the Lord. It is my prayer that you are begining to notice that the Word is in your thoughts on a more regular basis. Today, let's take time to thank God for all that He has done in our lives, for the Truth that He has shared with us and the Light He has given us for our path.

God I thank You for showing me that You are

_____

_____

_____

_____

God I thank You for what You have done

_____

_____

_____

_____

God I thank You for what I know You are doing

_____

_____

_____

_____

Go back to your favorite songs from this week and worship!!

Closing Prayer

Thank You God for loving me. Thank You for Your patience with me. I'm so thankful that You like to grow me. I worship You with my life today. In Jesus Name, Amen.

Devotional

Falling Back into Grace

Focus Scripture

Galatians 5:2-4

"Mark my words! I, Paul, tell you that if you let yourselves be circumcised, Christ will be of no value to you at all. Again, I declare to every man who lets himself be circumcised that he is obligated to obey the whole law. You who are trying to be justified by the law have been alienated from Christ; you have fallen away from grace."

Introduction

In the Old Testament, circumcision was an act of obedience for the Jewish people—God's chosen nation. It symbolized their covenant with Him and set them apart from the surrounding nations. But when Christ came, everything changed. Jesus' death on the cross brought salvation to all people, not just the Jews.

The early Christians faced tension. Many Jewish believers wanted the new Gentile converts to follow the old Jewish laws, including circumcision. But Paul boldly taught that salvation was no longer tied to fulfilling the law. He made it clear in Galatians 5:2-4 that relying on circumcision—or any other part of the law—meant turning away from grace.

Core Message

Paul wasn't just talking about circumcision. He was addressing a larger issue of self-righteousness and trying to earn salvation. It's not possible to obey the entire law perfectly, and that's why we need a Savior. Jesus paid the price for our sin, fulfilling the law's requirements and offering us the gift of grace.

When we act as though we can earn God's favor or salvation, we diminish the power of the cross. It's like telling Jesus, *"Thanks, but I've got this."* In doing so, we fall away from grace—not because God removes it, but because we stop trusting in it fully.

I know this because I've been there. I remember a time when I made a mistake—one that I knew better than to make. I immediately asked for forgiveness, but the weight of guilt and condemnation wouldn't lift. I couldn't understand why, especially since I was still reading my Bible daily and hearing from God in powerful ways.

One day, I finally asked the Lord why He would still speak to me and use me when I had failed Him. His answer cut straight to my heart: *"Did you ever think you were qualified?"*

In that moment, I realized something profound. Without even knowing it, I had started to believe that I had earned my standing with God. Sure, I wasn't perfect, but I thought I had been doing *"pretty well."* I had unknowingly built a foundation of self-righteousness, so when I needed to lean fully on His grace, I felt unworthy and condemned instead of free.

Paul's words in Galatians rang true in my life: when we depend on our works, we are obligated to keep the entire law. And none of us can—it is impossible. When we try to justify ourselves, we fall from grace, not because God's grace is removed, but because we turn away from depending on it.

That day, I confessed and repented of my prideful self-reliance. Instantly, God's love and mercy washed over me. I felt freedom for the first time in weeks because I had finally stepped back into grace.

Salvation is not about our works; it is about faith in what Jesus accomplished on the cross. When we truly rest in that truth, we experience His peace, love, and freedom in a way that changes everything.

Mind Shift

Take a moment to ask yourself:

- Are there areas in your life where you are trying to earn God's approval instead of resting in His grace?

- How does relying on God's grace change the way you approach your failures and successes?

Write down any thoughts or prayers, and commit to surrendering those self-reliant areas to God. Remind yourself daily that His grace is sufficient for you.

Your Mind Shift

_____

_____

_____

_____

Song Suggestion

"Broken Vessels (Amazing Grace)" by Hillsong Worship

This song beautifully reminds us that God's grace is enough for us, even in our brokenness. As you listen, let the lyrics remind you of the freedom we have in Christ.

Closing Prayer

Heavenly Father, thank You for the gift of grace. I confess the times I've tried to earn Your favor instead of trusting in the finished work of the cross. Forgive me for my pride and self-reliance. Help me to fully embrace Your grace, knowing that it is not by my works, but by faith in Jesus that I am saved. Thank You for loving me and calling me back into Your arms every time I fall short. In Jesus' name, Amen.

Devotional

The Fruit of Real Faith

Focus Scripture

James 2:14, 20-24

"What good is it, my brothers, if someone claims to have faith but has no deeds? Can such faith save them? ... You foolish person, do you want evidence that faith without deeds is useless? Was not our father Abraham considered righteous for what he did when he offered his son Isaac on the altar? You see that his faith and his actions were working together, and his faith was made complete by what he did. And the scripture was fulfilled that says, 'Abraham believed God, and it was credited to him as righteousness,' and he was called God's friend. You see that a person is considered righteous by what they do and not by faith alone."

Introduction

In our last devotional, we focused on the truth that we are saved by grace. We don't earn it, and we can't work hard enough to deserve it. Salvation comes through faith in Jesus' sacrifice on the cross. But then we come across James' words: *"Faith without works is dead,"* and it can feel a bit confusing, can't it?

Core Message

This passage has been misunderstood so many times. Some take it to mean that we must do something to earn our salvation, which directly conflicts with the message of grace. But James isn't saying that works save us. What he's teaching is that genuine faith produces evidence—fruit—that shows up in our actions.

Think about it this way: A branch doesn't bear fruit on its own. It can only grow fruit if it's connected to the vine. Jesus described Himself as the *true vine* (John 15:5). When we are connected to Him through faith, the fruit naturally begins to grow in our lives. This fruit—the good works, the kindness, the love, the sacrifices—comes from the Holy Spirit working in and through us. It's not something we manufacture on our own, and it's not something we use to prove ourselves to God.

James uses Abraham as an example of this truth. Abraham's faith wasn't just something he said or thought—it showed up in his actions. When God asked him to offer his son Isaac, Abraham trusted God completely, even when the command seemed impossible. His obedience demonstrated the faith he already had.

James 2:22 says, *"His faith and his actions were working together, and his faith was made complete by what he did."* Abraham's actions didn't create his faith; they revealed it. His works were the visible evidence of his trust in God.

It's the same for us. When we place our faith in Jesus, that faith changes us from the inside out. It impacts the way we think, speak, and act. Our actions—our *works*—become the overflow of a heart that is transformed by grace.

So, what does this mean for us today? It means we need to check our spiritual connection. Are we truly abiding in the vine? If we are, the fruit of the Spirit will naturally grow in our lives. Galatians 5:22-23 reminds us of what this fruit looks like: *love, joy, peace, patience, kindness, goodness, faithfulness, gentleness, and self-control.* These aren't things we can force or fake; they are evidence of the Spirit's work in us.

But let's not get it backward. Sometimes we try to produce the fruit ourselves. We think, *"If I do enough good things, God will love me more, or I'll feel more saved."* That's not how it works. We don't do good works to be saved; we do good works because we are saved. It's the difference between striving and abiding.

The works James talks about are not a burden—they are a joy. When we're connected to Jesus, serving others, loving deeply, and living righteously become natural outflows of our faith.

Faith without works is dead because it isn't real faith. Genuine faith changes us, and that change shows up in our lives. If you believe in Jesus, let that belief shine in your actions. Let your life be a testimony of the grace you've received.

Mind Shift

Ask yourself these questions:

- Is your faith bearing fruit? What evidence of God's work in your life can you see?

- Are you trying to "earn" God's approval through works, or are your works flowing from your faith in Him?

Spend time reflecting on your connection to the vine. If you feel distant, take time to abide in His presence through prayer, worship, and the Word. Remember, the fruit comes naturally when you're connected to the source.

Your Mind Shift

_____

_____

_____

_____

Song Suggestion

"Evidence" by Josh Baldwin

This song beautifully reminds us that the evidence of God's goodness and grace is all around us—and in us. Let it encourage you to trust Him and let His work show in your life.

Closing Prayer

Heavenly Father, thank You for saving me by grace through faith. Thank You for the gift of being connected to You, the true vine. Help me to trust You fully and to abide in You daily. May Your Spirit work in me and through me, producing fruit that brings glory to Your name. Forgive me for the times I've tried to do things on my own or to earn what You've already given freely. I surrender my heart and my actions to You, trusting that my faith will bear fruit as I remain in You. In Jesus' name, Amen.

Devotional

Love as Your First Fruit

Focus Scripture

Mark 12:30

Love the Lord with all your heart, with all your soul, with all your mind and with all your strength.

Introduction

Love is the first characteristic of the fruit of the Spirit, and it sets the tone for how we live our lives as followers of Christ. In Scripture, we're reminded to, *"Love the Lord your God with all your heart, with all your soul, with all your mind, and with all your strength"* (Mark 12:30). That kind of love is more than a fleeting feeling—it's a deep, lasting commitment.

Core Message

When I was 17, I made a deal with my mom. She wanted me to try a church with her. I agreed. However, on Saturday night, I wanted to stay out. I promised her that if she let me, I would still meet her in the morning for church. I kept my end of the bargain, even though I was nursing a hangover the next morning. I didn't know that walking into Otter Lake Church of the Nazarene that day would change everything. From the moment I walked in, I felt like I'd come home.

This wasn't my first encounter with God. When I was about seven years old, my family went to church together. I vividly remember coloring a picture of a seal on a rock while kneeling on the floor. That day, I prayed and asked Jesus into my heart. But not long after, we stopped going to church, and I didn't understand what having Jesus in my heart really meant.

At 17, it all made sense. Walking into that church, I realized what that prayer had been about. I had longed so much for my earthly father's acceptance that when I experienced the love of my heavenly Father, I clung to it with everything I had. That love was overwhelming, unconditional, and real.

From that point on, I was all in. I went to church every Sunday morning, Sunday night, Wednesday prayer meeting, and Thursday youth group. I read my Bible daily because I didn't want to lose the closeness I felt with God. His love was everything. *I was accepted by God! He loved me!*

I sang a song in church when I was seven called *No One Ever Cared for Me Like Jesus.* Years later, when I was 17, I sang another song called *With My Life in Your Hands.* There's a line in that song that says, *"With my life in Your hands, I can walk with head held high. It's a feeling I've dreamed of forever."* Those words captured what I felt—God's love made me feel whole.

That love also gave me strength to make hard choices, like letting go of my first love who had no interest in following Jesus. It wasn't easy, but God's love was worth it. It's been over 33 years since I fell in love with Jesus, and His love still amazes me. He still gives me butterflies and sweeps me off my feet. But I've learned that keeping that relationship alive takes intentionality.

In Revelation 2:4, God says, *"Yet I hold this against you: You have forsaken your first love. Remember the height from which you have fallen! Repent and do the things you did at first."* Those words are a sobering reminder that it's easy to let our love for God grow cold if we don't nurture it. I've had seasons where I had to force myself to sit down and read the Word or pray. But I'm so thankful I did because drifting away from God happens when we do nothing.

Christine Caine put it perfectly: *"To drift away from the Lord, you have to do nothing."* It's like any relationship—if you don't invest time, the connection weakens. God's voice doesn't change, but the noise of life can drown Him out. He's tender and kind, and He lets us feel the distance when we pull away—not to punish us, but to remind us to come back. And when we do, His arms are wide open, ready for us to fall in love with Him all over again.

Loving God first may not feel natural at the beginning of your walk with Him, but as you spend time with Him, that love will grow. He wants to be number one in your life, in your heart, and in your mind. When He is, everything else falls into place.

Mind Shift

Take some time to reflect on these questions:

1. Have you ever experienced the kind of love that only God can give? What was that moment like?

2. Is there anything in your life that's distracting you from keeping God as your first love?

3. What are some things you can do to rekindle your love for God and keep it alive?

Your Mind Shift

_____

_____

_____

_____

Song Suggestion

"With My Life in Your Hands" by Connie Scott

Spend some time listening to this song. Let the lyrics remind you of what it means to trust God completely and to live in the fullness of His love.

Closing Prayer

Dear Heavenly Father,

Thank You for loving me with an everlasting love. I want to love You with all my heart, soul, mind, and strength. Help me to keep You first in my life and to invest in our relationship daily. When I drift away, gently draw me back to You. Thank You for never giving up on me. I love You, Lord, and I want to fall more in love with You every day. In Jesus' name, Amen.

Devotional

Loving Your Neighbor as Yourself

Focus Scripture

Mark 12:31

The second is this: "Love your neighbor as yourself. There is no commandment greater than these."

Introduction

Today, we continue exploring love, one of the fruit of the Spirit. Yesterday, we focused on loving God, and now we turn to what it means to love your neighbor as yourself. But here's an essential question: how can we truly love others if we don't first love ourselves?

I grew up hearing all about loving other people, but no one ever talked about loving myself. A few years ago, during an inner healing prayer session at Centerpoint Church, I shared how I had always struggled to feel like I was enough. I carried this constant sense of inadequacy. The woman leading the session led me in a prayer asking God for forgiveness for believing the lie. I had never thought of it like that. I had been believing a lie.

When I believed lies about myself—things that God said weren't true—I was, in essence, choosing to trust my own opinion over His truth. That realization opened my eyes to how often I let negative self-talk drown out the voice of my heavenly Father. It was humbling, but it was also freeing.

Core Message

Over time, as I grew closer to the Lord, He began to show me how to see myself through His eyes. Let's compare our growth in faith to a child learning to walk. When a toddler stumbles and falls, we don't get angry or frustrated with them. We pick them up, encourage them, and celebrate their efforts. I understood that's how God sees us, and I could apply that grace to others. But it wasn't until I was about 40 years old that I finally learned to extend that same grace to myself.

Loving myself meant slowing down to face the choices I had made—the good intentions that had still caused pain, especially to my loved ones and children. As I learned to forgive myself something else happened. I was more easily able to give grace and understanding to those closest to me. I had been critical to them in the same way I saw me.

For years, I had no problem loving people in ministry. I could pour out love to the homeless, those battling addiction, teenagers in gangs, or women caught in prostitution. But when it came to my family, I struggled. I was critical of them in the same way I was critical of myself. The turning point came when I let God teach me how to love myself. Only then did I begin to love those closest to me with the tenderness and understanding they deserved.

Here's the key: Loving your neighbor as yourself starts with fully receiving God's love for you. When you accept His grace and allow His truth to shape your identity, it changes everything. Suddenly, your heart softens, and you begin to see others as He sees them. His love transforms how you relate to those closest to you.

God sees you as the apple of His eye. He delights over you and even sings over you (Zephaniah 3:17). Jesus chose to die for you so you could have a relationship with the Father. That selfless love is our model, and it empowers us to love others selflessly, too. But it all starts with letting God redefine how we see ourselves. When you let Him show you who you really are—cherished, forgiven, and chosen—His love will naturally overflow to those around you.

Mind Shift

Take some time to reflect on these questions:

1. What lies have you believed about yourself that don't align with God's truth?

2. How has God's grace changed the way you view yourself?

3. Who in your life needs to experience the same grace and compassion God has shown you?

Your Mind Shift

_____

_____

_____

_____

_____

_____

Song Suggestion

Spend some time listening to *Amazes Me* by Lincoln Brewster. Let the song remind you of the wonder of God's love for you and how it transforms your life and relationships.

Closing Prayer

Dear Heavenly Father,

Thank You for loving me so deeply and unconditionally. Forgive me for the times I've believed lies about myself instead of Your truth. Help me to see myself the way You see me—as loved, chosen, and cherished. Fill my heart with Your grace so I can love others with compassion and selflessness. Teach me to love my neighbor as myself by first accepting the fullness of Your love for me. In Jesus' name, Amen.

Devotional

Joy Beyond Circumstances

Focus Scripture

James 1:2

*tells us, "Consider it pure joy, my brothers and
sisters, whenever you face trials of many kinds,
because you know that the testing of your faith
produces perseverance."*

Introduction

Today, we move to *joy*, another beautiful characteristic of the fruit
of the Spirit. Joy is not about fleeting emotions or dependent on
the ups and downs of life. Instead, it's deeply rooted in the
assurance of God's presence and grace. It flows from recognizing
that God is actively working in our lives, even when we don't see
or understand it.

Joy is unique because it is grounded in God's promises, not in our
circumstances. James 1:2 says, *"Consider it pure joy, my brothers
and sisters, whenever you face trials of many kinds, because you*

174

know that the testing of your faith produces perseverance." At first, this verse baffled me. How can you be joyful during trials? But as I've walked through difficult seasons, I've come to understand—it's not about being thankful for the hard times themselves. It's about finding gratitude and assurance in God's presence *through* them.

Core Message

I've learned that joy is tied to trust. It's trusting that God is faithful, even when life feels unbearable. Romans 8:28 reminds us, *"We know that in all things God works for the good of those who love Him, who have been called according to His purpose."* That verse doesn't say everything will be good, but it promises that God will bring good *from* even the most painful situations. That is where joy is found—not in pretending everything is okay, but in believing that God is with us and His grace will carry us through.

A few years ago, I heard Beth Moore say something that really stuck with me. She said that just because God *can* bring good from something doesn't mean we wouldn't trade that situation if we could. That resonated with me so deeply. There are moments in my life I wish had gone differently, heartaches I would gladly exchange. Yet, even in those moments, I've experienced the steady presence of God and the reassurance that nothing is wasted in His hands.

I think back to times when joy felt impossible, like during seasons of deep loss and disappointment. It wasn't happiness I clung to—it was the knowledge that God was still working. Joy doesn't erase pain, but it gives us the strength to endure it. It reminds us that even in the hardest times, God's grace is enough.

I want to encourage you to pause today and think about God's goodness in your life. Where have you seen His faithfulness? How has His grace carried you through seasons when you felt like giving up? Let those moments be a reminder that *He is the source of true joy.*

Mind Shift

Take a moment to reflect on these questions:

1. Can you think of a time when you felt joy despite difficult circumstances? What gave you that sense of peace and assurance?

2. How does the promise of Romans 8:28 give you hope in your current situation?

3. In what ways can you lean into God's presence and experience His joy today?

Your Mind Shift

_____

_____

_____

_____

Song Suggestion

Spend time listening to *Joy* by For King & Country. Let the song remind you of the power of choosing joy, even in the face of trials, and the hope we have in Christ.

Closing Prayer

Dear Heavenly Father,

Thank You for the gift of joy that is so much deeper than happiness. Help me to trust You in every situation, even when it feels overwhelming. Teach me to see Your hand at work, even in the hard places. Thank You for the promise that You bring good from everything, no matter how broken it may seem. Fill my heart with Your joy and let it strengthen me to face today with hope. In Jesus' name, Amen.

Day 41

Growing Your Roots

Here we go! It has been another week! How exciting to be joining with God in His work within us. Let's look back at what God has been shifting in our minds.

Lord Jesus grow some roots in us to keep us stable on this journey. In Jesus Name, Amen.

1. Falling Back Into Grace: Galatians 5:2-4 "Mark my words! I, Paul, tell you that if you let yourselves be circumcised, Christ will be of no value to you at all. Again, I declare to every man who lets himself be circumcised that he is obligated to obey the whole law. You who are trying to be justified by the law have been alienated from Christ; you have fallen away from grace."

Your Mind Shift

_____

_____

_____

_____

2. The Fruit of Real Faith: James 2:14, 20-24

"What good is it, my brothers, if someone claims to have faith but has no deeds? Can such faith save them? … You foolish person, do you want evidence that faith without deeds is useless? Was not our father Abraham considered righteous for what he did when he offered his son Isaac on the altar? You see that his faith and his actions were working together, and his faith was made complete by what he did. And the scripture was fulfilled that says, 'Abraham believed God, and it was credited to him as righteousness,' and he was called God's friend. You see that a person is considered righteous by what they do and not by faith alone."

Your Mind Shift

_____

_____

_____

_____

3. Love as Your First Fruit: Mark 12:30 Love the Lord your God with all your heart and with all your soul and with all your mind and with all your strength.

Your Mind Shift

_____

_____

_____

_____

4. Love Your Neighbor as Yourself: Mark 12:31 "The second is this: "Love your neighbor as yourself. There is no commandment greater than these."

Your Mind Shift

_____

_____

_____

_____

5. Joy Beyond Your Circumstances: James 1:2 tells us, "Consider it pure joy, my brothers and sisters, whenever you face trials of many kinds, because you know that the testing of your faith produces perseverance."

Your Mind Shift

_____

_____

_____

_____

Which Mind Shift do you feel the Holy Spirit leading you to focus on again today? Reread that devotional and write any new insights that you need to remember below.

_____

_____

_____

_____

Closing Prayer

Lord My God I thank You for Your amazing grace that saves me.
Please Lord remind my heart that my faith in Your Son's blood on
the cross is the only righteousness that saves me. As I grow in Your
Love and Truth please remind me that I have fruit in my life only
from You! It is not my works that save me. Please Lord keep my
confidence in Your sacrifice and not my works. Your love for me,
my love for You and Your love flowing out of me to others around
me is so beautiful. Keep doing that in me. Help me keep my eyes
on You and my confidence that You are at work in all things in my
life. God You are love. Make me love too. In Jesus Name, Amen.

Day 42

Finishing the Week In Worship

Another amazing day to give thanks to the Lord for all that He has done and is doing in our lives. He is worthy.

Lord please open our eyes today as we ask ourselves these questions. Please help me to see You all throughout my life and all around me. In Jesus Name, Amen.

God I thank You for showing me that You are

_____

_____

_____

_____

God I thank You for what You have done

_____

_____

_____

_____

God I thank You for what I know You are doing

_____

_____

_____

_____

Go back to your favorite songs from this week and worship!!

Closing Prayer

Lord Jesus so many beautiful Truths that You have been writing on my heart. Keep transforming my mind. I want these Truths to grow deep within me. When pressure is placed on me, my hearts desire is that the evidence of You in my life would be seen. I thank You for never giving up on me. In Jesus Name, Amen.

Devotional

Peace All the Time

Focus Scripture

Isaiah 26:3

*"You will keep in perfect peace those whose
minds are steadfast, because they trust in you."*

Introduction

Today, we're reflecting on *peace*, another beautiful characteristic
of the fruit of the Spirit. Peace doesn't mean life is free from
storms; it's about having a deep, steady calm within, no matter
what is happening around you.

One of my favorite pictures of peace in Scripture is Jesus sleeping
in the boat during the storm. The disciples were panicking,
frantically waking Him up, but Jesus remained calm. He wasn't
worried about the wind or waves because He trusted completely in
the Father. That's the kind of peace I want—the kind that allows
me to rest, no matter what's happening.

Core Message

There was a season in my life when anxiety felt like a constant companion. Psalm 3:5–7 became my lifeline: *"I lie down and sleep; I wake again, because the Lord sustains me."* Those words reminded me that I didn't have to carry the weight of the world on my shoulders. God is the one who holds everything together, and because of that, I can rest.

One moment stands out when I felt God's peace in an extraordinary way. I was on vacation in Traverse City, sitting by the bay with my Bible and a cup of coffee, my baseball cap pulled low. The wind was fierce, creating white-capped waves on the water. As I sat there, reading and praying, I thought of Peter stepping out onto the water during a storm. God whispered to my heart, showing me that peace isn't about the absence of waves— it's about trusting Him enough to keep walking.

After my quiet time, I started walking back to my car. As I crossed a dip in the ground, the wind stopped completely. Moments before, it had been blowing so hard that I had to hold onto my hat and notebook. Now, it was completely still. I froze, stunned by the sudden stillness. The waves still rolled in, but the wind was gone. I stepped back toward the water, and the wind started again. When I returned to the dip, the stillness came back.

In that moment, God showed me something so sweet: *Life will always have storms, but I can carry His peace within me wherever I go.*

That wasn't the only time I've experienced His peace. You might remember when I shared about selling my business. That was the first time I felt a deep sense of peace in the middle of chaos. Since then, I've learned to go back to Philippians 4:6–7 whenever I feel overwhelmed:

"Do not be anxious about anything, but in every situation, by prayer and petition, with thanksgiving, present your requests to God. And the peace of God, which transcends all understanding, will guard your hearts and your minds in Christ Jesus."

That verse is so much more than a comforting promise—it's an invitation to shift our perspective. When we release our fears to God and thank Him for all He's already done, His peace fills the spaces where anxiety once lived. It doesn't mean we won't feel pain, frustration, or even tears. But it does mean we can rest in the knowledge that God is with us and His peace is real.

One of my favorite quotes about peace is from Corrie ten Boom: *"Worry does not empty tomorrow of its sorrow. It empties today of its strength."* Peace allows us to focus on God instead of our circumstances. It reminds us that He is in control, even when life feels overwhelming.

186

As you reflect today, I hope you're encouraged to take those *mind shift* moments where God speaks to your heart. He wants to change how you see the storms in your life so you can experience His peace in every season. Whether life feels calm or chaotic, His peace is always available to you.

Mind Shift

Take a moment to reflect on these questions:

1. What storms in your life are challenging your peace?

2. How can you anchor yourself in God's promises today?

3. What does it look like for you to carry God's peace, no matter the circumstances?

Your Mind Shifts

_____

_____

_____

_____

Song Suggestion

Spend time listening to *Peace Be Still* by The Belonging Co. featuring Lauren Daigle. Let the song remind you to rest in God's peace and trust Him, even in the storms of life.

Closing Prayer

Dear Heavenly Father,

Thank You for being my peace in every moment of my life—during the storms and in the calm. Teach me to trust You completely and rest in Your promises. Help me to release my anxieties to You and hold onto Your Word. Thank You for a peace that goes beyond my understanding and for always being with me. In Jesus' name, Amen.

Devotional

Patience in the Waiting

Focus Scripture

Romans 8:25

"But if we hope for what we do not see, we wait for it with patience."

Introduction

Patience—this might be everyone's least favorite characteristic of the fruit of the Spirit. In fact, it's often translated as "long-suffering," which doesn't exactly sound appealing. Patience means waiting, and in our fast-paced world, waiting can feel unbearable. We want everything now, and even "now" sometimes feels too slow. But patience is necessary for growth, and God often uses the waiting seasons to shape us in ways we can't see.

Patience makes me think about the rhythm of the seasons. Spring is filled with fresh growth. Summer brings steady progress, and everything is green and thriving. By fall, we see the harvest—the fruit that was nurtured throughout the year. But then comes winter, when everything appears dead. In Michigan, where I live, winter can feel endless. The trees are bare, the grass is brown, and the cold seems to last forever. It's easy to think nothing is happening.

Core Message

One winter day, I noticed small knobs on the branches of a tree in my yard. They didn't seem like much at first glance, but the Holy Spirit nudged me to pay attention. Later, I went inside and researched tree growth. What I learned amazed me: those tiny knobs held everything the branch needed to grow when spring arrived. During the winter, the tree wasn't dead—it was just working internally, storing up what it needed for the next season.

That's what patience often looks like in our lives. Sometimes, we're in a winter season where nothing seems to be happening on the outside. It's tempting to feel stuck or discouraged, but God is doing deep, internal work in us during those times. He's preparing us for what's next, even if we can't see it yet.

It's important to remember that patience isn't just about waiting. It's about how we wait. Patience is deeply connected to the other characteristics of the fruit of the Spirit. The love we have for God, the grace we extend to ourselves and others, the joy we find in His faithfulness, and the peace we cling to in the storms—all of these can strengthen us in times of waiting.

I've found that patience also requires trust. Trusting that God's timing is perfect, even when it feels delayed. Trusting that He knows what He's doing, even when we don't understand. Romans 8:25 reminds us, "If we hope for what we do not see, we wait for it with patience." Hope and patience go hand in hand. When we trust that God is working, even in the unseen, we can wait with confidence instead of frustration.

One of the most encouraging truths about patience is that winter is never the final season. Spring always comes. The trees bud, flowers bloom, and life begins to show again. The same is true in our spiritual lives. The waiting seasons aren't wasted. God is preparing us for something new, and the fruit will come in time.

As you reflect today, think about the places in your life where you feel like you're in a winter season. Maybe you're waiting for an answer, a breakthrough, or a new direction. Remember that God is still at work, even when it feels like nothing is happening. He's growing something in you that will show in its season.

Mind Shift

Take a moment to reflect on these questions:

1. Are there areas in your life where God is asking you to wait? How does it feel?

2. What would it look like to trust Him fully during this season?

3. How can you focus on the internal growth God is doing in you right now?

Your Mind Shift

_____

_____

_____

_____

Song Suggestion

Spend time listening to *In The Middle by Isaac Carree*. Let the lyrics remind you of God's faithfulness in every season and His perfect timing.

Closing Prayer

Dear Heavenly Father,

Thank You for being with me in every season of life. Help me to trust You when I feel like nothing is happening. Remind me that You are working, even in the waiting, and that You are growing something beautiful within me. Teach me to have patience and to hold onto the hope of what You have promised. Thank You for the assurance that spring will come. In Jesus' name, Amen.

Devotional

Kindness, A Gentle Gift

Focus Scripture

Ephesians 4:29

"Do not let any unwholesome talk come out of your mouths, but only what is helpful for building others up according to their needs, that it may benefit those who listen."

Introduction

Kindness is today's characteristic of the fruit of the Spirit. I'll admit, at first, I wanted to combine it with goodness because they seem so similar. But the more I've reflected on kindness, the more I've realized how essential and unique it is. Kindness is more than a surface-level action—it's a disposition, a steady and tender love that reflects the heart of God.

Kindness reminds me of the love and patience we've already talked about. Like love, kindness is rooted in covenantal loyalty—it's steadfast and intentional. And like patience, it requires a softness that doesn't always come naturally. I've come to realize that kindness isn't just about what we do; it's about who we're becoming as we stay connected to the *true vine*, Jesus.

Core Message

Florence Littauer's book *Silver Boxes* offers a beautiful picture of kindness. She compares our words to gifts, like silver boxes wrapped with bows. She encourages us to be careful with our words, making sure they build others up rather than tearing them down. Ephesians 4:29 perfectly captures this idea, reminding us that our words should benefit those who hear them. That's not always easy, though, is it? Sometimes, we want to get straight to the point, especially when we're dealing with hard truths. But kindness mellows the harshness of life. It's what makes those hard truths easier to accept.

I've noticed in myself that kindness requires me to be purposeful. I remember a time when my best friend teased me about how I don't do small talk. I laughed it off, but her words stayed with me. I started to pay attention to how often I jump straight into deep, challenging conversations, skipping over the gentle, relational parts of communication. Kindness, I've learned, often looks like slowing down and softening my approach—choosing to be fully present with someone before diving into the serious stuff.

I love that Jesus does this with me. He doesn't rush into the hard conversations. Instead, He takes time to meet me where I am, tenderly preparing my heart before addressing what needs to change. That's the kind of kindness I want to reflect in my relationships—with others and with myself.

Kindness isn't always easy, especially when we're tired, hurt, or frustrated. But the beautiful thing about this fruit of the Spirit is that it doesn't come from us—it comes from staying connected to Jesus. When we abide in Him, His kindness flows through us. It's not something we have to muster up on our own.

I love this simple poem by George Herbert that captures the heart of kindness:

"Be soft, even if you stand tall.

Be kind, even if others are cruel.

Be light, even when the world feels dark.

Be love, because that's who He is."

Kindness is a gift we give to others, but it's also something we receive from God. When I think about His kindness in my own life, I'm reminded of how tender He has been with me in every season. It challenges me to offer the same tenderness to those around me.

Mind Shift

Take some time to reflect on these questions:

1. Are your words building others up, like silver boxes with bows, or are they tearing others down?

2. How can you show kindness today, even in small and simple ways?

3. In what areas of your life do you need to let God's kindness soften your heart?

Your Mind Shifts

_____

_____

_____

_____

Song Suggestion

Song Suggestion: Revolutionary by Josh Wilson

Closing Prayer

Dear Heavenly Father,

Thank You for Your unfailing kindness toward me. Teach me to reflect Your heart in my words and actions. Help me to soften, to slow down, and to listen with love. Fill me with Your Spirit so that Your kindness flows through me to those around me. Remind me to be kind not only to others but also to myself. Thank You for meeting me with gentleness and preparing my heart for Your truth. In Jesus' name, Amen.

Devotional

Goodness, The Courage to Love Well

Focus Scripture

Romans 12:9

"Let love be genuine. Abhor what is evil; hold fast to what is good."

Introduction

Today, we're talking about *goodness*, a characteristic of the fruit of the Spirit that often gets overlooked but is essential in our walk with God. Goodness is more than being kind or doing the right thing—it's a brightness in heart and life, rooted in love and truth. It's about standing firm in what is right while still extending grace and compassion.

When I think about goodness, it reminds me of how love shows up in action. *Real love doesn't shy away from hard things.* Goodness is the courage to hold others accountable, to lovingly speak truth, and to protect what matters most. It goes beyond kindness. Where kindness softens and builds trust, goodness sometimes needs to challenge, correct, or set boundaries—but always out of love.

Core Message

I'll never forget a moment when goodness showed up in my parenting. Taylor, my oldest daughter, was about five or six years old at the time. Her grandparents lived next door and had a deep pond in their yard. Taylor has always loved the water, so we made a rule that she could never go near the pond without a life jacket. It didn't matter if it was the middle of winter—the rule was the rule.

One day, after Taylor's grandparents had moved, a new family moved in with a little girl the same age as her. Taylor was thrilled to have a friend next door and couldn't wait to play with her. I reluctantly agreed to let her go over, but a little while later, I noticed the girls weren't playing near the neighbor's house. Panic set in as I imagined the worst. I yelled for her dad to call the neighbor while I ran across the yard, fearing they had gone into the pond.

When I got there, I saw Taylor and her friend standing in the shallow part of the pond. Relief and frustration washed over me. I called her over, and as we walked home, I cried. When we got back to the house, I sat Taylor down and told her she was going to get a spanking. With tears running down my face, I explained that she could have drowned. The spanking wasn't about anger—it was about love. I wanted her to remember the seriousness of the situation so she would be safe in the future.

That moment taught me so much about goodness. *Goodness is doing the hard thing because you love someone enough to protect them, even if it's painful.* It's about balancing grace and truth, kindness and accountability.

This characteristic of the fruit of the Spirit is vital in relationships. Whether it's in mentoring, parenting, or sharing God's Word, goodness helps us navigate those moments when love requires us to speak up, set boundaries, or enforce consequences. It reminds me of Romans 12:9, which says, *"Let love be genuine. Abhor what is evil; hold fast to what is good."* Genuine love doesn't ignore the truth; it holds fast to what is good, even when it's uncomfortable.

Goodness also requires us to be anchored in God's love and compassion. When we understand how much we need His grace, it allows us to extend that same grace to others. But extending grace doesn't mean avoiding hard conversations or consequences. Instead, it means approaching them with love, empathy, and humility.

Here's a truth I've come to learn: *goodness isn't about being "good enough."* It's about reflecting God's heart in the way we live and love. When we are deeply connected to Him, His goodness flows through us. We are able to love well—not because we're perfect, but because He is.

I love this quote by C.S. Lewis: *"Love is something more stern and splendid than mere kindness."* Goodness is love in action—it's steadfast and courageous, willing to do what's right even when it's hard. It's a love that protects, corrects, and guides with tenderness and truth.

Mind Shift

Take a moment to reflect on these questions:

1. Is there someone in your life who needs you to show goodness by lovingly speaking truth or setting boundaries?

2. How can you balance grace and accountability in your relationships?

3. In what areas of your life do you need to rely on God's strength to reflect His goodness?

Your Mind Shift

_____

_____

_____

_____

Song Suggestion

Listen to *Goodness of God* by Bethel Music. Let the song remind you of God's unfailing goodness in your life and inspire you to reflect that same goodness to others.

Closing Prayer

Dear Heavenly Father,

Thank You for Your steadfast goodness in my life. Teach me to reflect Your heart in the way I love others. Help me to be tender and compassionate while also being courageous enough to speak truth. Anchor me in Your love so that I can give grace and accountability in equal measure. Thank You for showing me what goodness looks like through Your faithfulness. Help me to live in a way that points others to You. In Jesus' name, Amen.

Devotional

Gentleness: The Quiet Strength

Focus Scripture

Galatians 5:25

Since we live by the Spirit, let us keep in step with the Spirit.

Introduction

Gentleness was the last thing I wanted to hear about when I first became a Christian. I was strong, independent, and loud. Being gentle felt weak, almost powerless, and I wasn't interested in being either. I thought God would want me to use my boldness, my independence, my voice—not quiet them. But as I grew in my faith, I realized I didn't understand gentleness at all. I was so wrong.

Gentleness isn't weakness. It's restrained power. It's strength under control, guided by the Spirit of God.

203

Core Message

I wish I could say I grasped this truth right away, but it took time. Another word I wrestled with was *submission*. I didn't like it. Submission felt like giving up my independence, like surrendering who I was. But God patiently worked on my heart. He showed me that submission to Him is not about losing freedom but *gaining* it. It's voluntarily placing my life in His hands, trusting that He knows me better than I know myself. He knows my fears, my strengths, and even my stubbornness. And now, I can honestly say I happily surrender to His authority because I trust Him completely.

One of the most beautiful illustrations of gentleness I've ever heard is the image of a wild Mustang being tamed. A Mustang is powerful, full of untamed energy and strength. But when it learns to trust its master, something beautiful happens. The horse doesn't lose its power—it learns to direct it. It becomes attuned to the master's voice, responding to even the smallest nudge or quietest command.

That's gentleness. It's strength under submission, power guided by trust. The Mustang is protected, loved, cared for, and most assuredly able to fulfill its purpose.

This is what I long for in my life. I want to live so attuned to God's Spirit that I respond to His smallest whisper. I want to be divinely distracted by Him, walking in step with His Spirit every moment of every day. That's the heart of this devotional and the life I'm pursuing. It's not about doing everything perfectly but about staying close enough to hear His voice and trusting Him enough to obey it.

That's what our focus verse is talking about:

"Since we live by the Spirit, let us keep in step with the Spirit." – Galatians 5:25

I love that imagery. It reminds me that walking with God is not about rushing ahead with my plans or dragging my feet in doubt. It's about moving with Him, trusting His timing, and leaning into His wisdom. And honestly, it's in those moments of trust that I've experienced the most peace. *He knows what's ahead, and He knows what I need to get there.*

I think about a time years ago when I was teaching children's church. To help the kids understand what it means to follow God's voice, I blindfolded two of them and assigned each a leader. The leaders were supposed to guide them through a course in the room using only their voices. But there was a catch. The other kids were told to yell out distractions and try to confuse the blindfolded ones. The goal was for the blindfolded kids to know their leader's voice and obey it over all the others.

Life can feel a lot like that room full of noise. There are distractions everywhere, voices pulling us in a hundred different directions. Fear, doubt, pride, and even our own plans can make it hard to hear God's voice. But gentleness requires us to slow down, tune out the noise, and listen closely. *It's about knowing His voice and yielding to it.*

And trust me, I'm still learning. There are moments when I want to push ahead, to make things happen in my own strength. Sometimes, I still go ahead on my own for a minute. When I exhaust myself from trying it on my own, God is waiting to take the lead again. As I grow closer to the Lord through all of life, I learn to trust and obey Him more quickly and consistently.

That's gentleness—being so in tune with His voice that I respond *in step* with Him.

There's an old hymn I used to sing as a child that still echoes in my heart today:

"Trust and obey, for there's no other way

To be happy in Jesus, but to trust and obey."

Those words sum up what gentleness means. It's about trusting God completely and obeying His leading, knowing He knows the way. It's about submitting my strength, my plans, and my voice to Him because I know He is good, and I know His ways are perfect.

Mind Shift

Take some time today to reflect on gentleness in your own life. Are there areas where God is asking you to surrender your strength to Him? Maybe it's in a relationship, a decision, or even in the way you speak to yourself. Ask Him to help you hear His voice above the noise and trust Him to lead you. Remember, gentleness isn't about losing yourself—it's about letting God guide your strength.

Your Mind Shift

_____

_____

_____

_____

Song Suggestion

Before we close in prayer, take a moment to listen to *"I Surrender All"* by CeCe Winans. Let the words remind you of the beauty and freedom that come from submitting your life to God.

Closing Prayer

Father, thank You for teaching me the beauty of gentleness. Thank You for showing me that gentleness isn't about weakness but about trusting You with my strength. Help me to stay in step with Your Spirit, to hear Your voice over the noise, and to respond with quiet confidence in Your love. May my life reflect Your goodness and bring glory to Your name. In Jesus' name, amen.

Day 48

Growing Your Roots

1. Peace All The Time: Isaiah 26:3 You will keep in perfect peace those whose minds are steadfast, because they trust in you."

Your Mind Shift

_____

_____

_____

_____

2. Patience In The Waiting: Romans 8:25 "But if we hope for what we do not see, we wait for it with patience."

Your Mind Shift

_____

_____

_____

_____

3. Kindness, A Gentle Gift: Ephesians 4:29 "Do not let any unwholesome talk come out of your mouths, but only what is

helpful for building others up according to their needs, that it may benefit those who listen."

Your Mind Shift

_____

_____

_____

_____

4. Goodness, The Courage To Love Well: Romans 12:9 "Let love be genuine. Abhor what is evil; hold fast to what is good."

Your Mind Shift

_____

_____

_____

_____

5. Gentleness, The Quiet Strength: Galatians 5:25 Since we live by the Spirit, let us keep in step with the Spirit.

Your Mind Shift

_____

_____

_____

_____

Which of these mind shifts needs some extra focus? Ask the Holy Spirit to show you which one you need to think about and reread that devotional for today. Below write any new thoughts or things that you need to remember.

_____

_____

_____

_____

_____

Closing Prayer

Lord God, I come to You today knowing that the only way to have these fruits in my life is to stay connected to you. You are the One that fills me up. Help me do my part and keep these mind shifts at the front of my mind. As I stay close to You and learn to hear Your Voice more and more I know that peace will be a part of my everyday life and patience will begin to show up more and more. Keep me attentive and obedient to Your Voice and encourage me Lord as I learn to be both kind and good to both myself and to those around me. That obedience to Your Voice is gentleness and courage. Yes Lord I want to walk boldly weather that means restraining myself when I hear You tell me to be quiet or speaking truth into someones life. Thank You for working through me even when I mess up. Only You Lord. I'm all Yours. In Jesus Name, Amen.

Day 49

Finishing the Week In Worship

Another week of getting to know the amazing God we serve and to allow His Truths to penetrate our minds and transform the very way we see everything. Today begin with prayer asking God to show you all that you have to be grateful for.

God I thank You for showing me that You are

_____

_____

_____

_____

God I thank You for what You have done

_____

_____

_____

_____

God I thank You for what I know You are doing

_____

_____

_____

_____

Go back to your favorite songs from this week and worship!!

Closing Prayer

Lord I am truely thankful for having You in my life. You fill me with love and forgive my shortcomings. Thank You for all of the blessings that I have listed above. You are so good to me. In Jesus Name. Amen.

Devotional

Faithfulness: My Steady Anchor

Focus Scripture

---

2 Timothy 2: 13

If we are faithless, He remains faithful, for He cannot disown Himself.

Introduction

When I think about *faithfulness*, my heart instantly turns to God. For 33 years, He has been my steady. Through every storm and every triumph, He has been there, unchanging. His faithfulness is woven into every corner of my life, even in moments when I wasn't paying attention. I can't count the times He's carried me through heartbreak, guided me through confusion, or waited patiently while I tried to do things my own way. *He is my constant—the One I can always rely on.*

But when Paul talks about faithfulness as a fruit of the Spirit in Galatians 5:22-23, he isn't just describing God's faithfulness to us. He's asking if *we* are faithful. Am I faithful? Am I steady? Am I trustworthy? Can people count on me the way I count on God? And even deeper—does my life show that I truly believe Him?

Core Message

Faithfulness isn't just about being dependable in the eyes of others. *It's about living out what we claim to believe.* Do I really trust that when God says my sins are washed whiter than snow, it's true? Do I live like this world isn't my home, like heaven is my real destination? Do I hold tightly to His promises, even when life feels unsteady? *Faithfulness is the evidence of that belief.* It's not just saying we trust God; it's showing it.

I want to be found faithful to the One who has never once wavered in His faithfulness to me. But I'd be lying if I said I don't struggle. There are days when my faith feels small. Days when I'm overwhelmed by fear or doubt.

There's a story in Mark 9 that I hold close on those days. A father brings his son to Jesus, desperate for healing, and he says to Him, *"I do believe; help me overcome my unbelief!"* (Mark 9:24). I love that. It's so real, so honest. That father *believed,* but he also knew he needed Jesus to fill in the gaps where his faith fell short. I pray that prayer often: *"Lord, I believe, but help me where I'm struggling to believe."*

The beauty is that God doesn't reject us when our faith is fragile. He meets us right where we are and gently grows our trust in Him. He's done that for me time and time again. I think about the Israelites in the wilderness and how God used manna to teach them to trust Him. He provided just enough for each day and told them not to store any extra. Some of them couldn't help themselves. They tried to collect more, worried there wouldn't be enough the next day. But God was patient. He kept showing up, providing day after day, teaching them that He could be trusted.

That's what faithfulness looks like—it's *daily trust,* even when you don't have all the answers. And God is so gracious to give us opportunities to practice it. I've seen Him use small moments in my life to stretch my faith. There was a season when I prayed for something so deeply, and His answer didn't come the way I expected. I felt let down at first, but as I kept leaning into Him, I began to see His hand in the outcome. Looking back, I can see that *His plan was so much better than mine.*

That's the kind of faithfulness I want to live with—the kind that trusts Him even when things don't make sense.

Faithfulness is about being *steady* in your belief and living in a way that reflects it. It's about being a person who can be relied on, not just by others but by God. Are we living lives that say, *"God, You can trust me to follow Your Word, to obey Your voice, to love the people You've placed in my life"*? That's what I ask myself when I think about this fruit of the Spirit.

And the beautiful thing is that faithfulness doesn't grow from striving. *It grows from abiding.*

Jesus said in John 15:4, *"Remain in me, as I also remain in you. No branch can bear fruit by itself; it must remain in the vine."* Faithfulness flows from staying close to Him. When we spend time in His presence, His Spirit works in us, growing the fruit of faithfulness naturally. It's not about setting impossible goals to be perfect. It's about leaning into Him and letting His faithfulness inspire ours.

I want to leave you with this: If you're struggling to trust God fully, if there are parts of your heart where belief comes easily and others where doubt creeps in, *that's okay.* You're not alone. Pray the prayer of the father in Mark 9:24. Be honest with God about where you're struggling, and let Him grow your faith step by step.

He's patient, and He's faithful.

And He'll meet you exactly where you are.

Mind Shift

Take a moment to think about your own faithfulness. Are there areas in your life where God is calling you to trust Him more deeply? Is your faith in His promises reflected in the way you live? Ask Him to show you where He's inviting you to grow. Remember, faithfulness doesn't come from trying harder—it comes from staying close to Him.

Your Mind Shift

_____

_____

_____

_____

Song Suggestion

Listen to *"Faithful and True"* by Steven Curtis Chapman. Let the lyrics remind you of God's unchanging faithfulness and encourage you to live in a way that reflects your trust in Him.

Closing Prayer

Lord, thank You for being my steady, my constant, and my anchor. You are always faithful, even when I fall short. Help me to trust You more deeply and to live in a way that reflects my faith. Teach me to be steady, to be reliable, and to live with a faithfulness that honors You. Grow my belief in Your promises and help me to be

faithful to You, just as You have been faithful to me. In Jesus'
name, amen.

Devotional

Self-Control: Saying No to Say Yes

---

2 Timothy 1:9 "For God did not give us a spirit of fear, but of love, power and self-control."

Introduction

Self-control is the final characteristic in the fruit of the Spirit, and for me, it's one of the hardest. It's the true mastery of oneself—learning to tell yourself *no* so you can say *yes* to something better. That's what self-control has come to mean for me: the strength to say *no* to myself, even when every part of me wants to give in, because I know that saying *no* is the first step to keeping my heart aligned with God.

I'll never forget a Bible study I did years ago on the book of *Daniel* by Beth Moore. At the beginning of the study, we were asked to fast from something for the duration of the course. The idea was to draw inspiration from Daniel, Shadrach, Meshach, and Abednego,

221

who refused the king's food and instead chose vegetables and water.

Core Message

Fasting can teach us a lot about self-control, and I knew right away it wasn't going to be easy. It was literally the practice of saying *no* to my flesh. *Goodness, we need to practice that.*

I remember one particular test of self-control during a camping trip with some friends. At the time, I had only my two daughters, and we were camping with friends who weren't believers. I knew the evenings around the campfire would be filled with drinking and indulgence, and I felt the pull of temptation even before the trip began. I prayed about it, and God led me to fast from chocolate while on our trip.

Now, fasting from chocolate while camping might not sound like a big deal to some, but for me, it was a sacrifice. My favorite part of camping is making s'mores, and to me, a s'more without chocolate is no s'more at all. Every evening, after the kids were in bed and the adults started drinking, I felt that tug in my heart. I wanted a s'more so badly. But every time I told myself *no*, I found my focus shifting back to God. That simple act of self-denial reminded me why I was fasting—to keep my eyes on Him, to strengthen my witness to those around me, and to lean into His power instead of my own.

That camping trip taught me something profound about self-control. *It's not about depriving yourself for the sake of deprivation. It's about focusing your attention on what matters most.* Saying *no* to the temporary allows you to say *yes* to the eternal. For me, every denied craving for chocolate was a small victory that gave me the strength to resist bigger temptations. God used that seemingly small act of obedience to keep my heart anchored in Him.

I've also seen how self-control weaves into other aspects of the fruit of the Spirit. It's connected to gentleness, patience, and even joy. As I've learned to listen to God's voice, I've seen how every *no* He asks of me is for my good. *He never tells us no to something that will benefit us.* Instead, He's always leading us toward what will grow us and bring Him glory. Learning to say *no* isn't about punishment—it's about protection and purpose.

One area where I've wrestled most with self-control is in my mouth and my mind. I used to think I couldn't control my thoughts or words, but the truth is, I was letting them control me. Over time, as I've stayed more connected to the Holy Spirit, I've learned to *boss my mind around* (as I like to call it) and make it obedient to Christ. When I tell my mind to focus on God's truth instead of my fears or frustrations, peace follows. And when I let Him guard my words, the fruit of gentleness and kindness begins to show in my relationships.

As we come to the end of this study on the fruit of the Spirit, I want to remind you of something important: *the fruit isn't something we can produce on our own.* A branch doesn't bear fruit by trying harder; it bears fruit by staying connected to the vine.

In the same way, we don't grow in self-control—or love, joy, peace, or any of the other fruit—by setting rigid goals or striving in our own strength. Instead, we grow by *abiding* in Christ. When we live in His presence, spend time in His Word, and stay tuned to His voice, the fruit shows up naturally.

Jesus said in John 15:5, *"I am the vine; you are the branches. If you remain in me and I in you, you will bear much fruit; apart from me you can do nothing."*

That's the key to self-control. It's not about white-knuckling your way through temptation or forcing yourself to be better. *It's about staying close to Jesus and letting His Spirit do the work in you.* When you abide in Him, self-control isn't something you have to manufacture. *It's something He produces in you.*

Mind Shift

Where is God asking you to practice self-control? Maybe it's in your habits, your thoughts, or even your words. Take a moment to ask Him to show you where He's inviting you to say no so you can say yes to something better. And remember, it's not about trying harder—it's about staying connected to Him.

Your Mind Shift

_____

_____

_____

_____

Song Suggestion

Listen to *"Turn Your Eyes Upon Jesus"* by Lauren Daigle. Let the words remind you to shift your focus back to Him, trusting that He will give you the strength you need to live a life of self-control.

Closing Prayer

Lord, thank You for teaching me the beauty of self-control. Help me to see that every no is an opportunity to say yes to You. Teach me to stay connected to You, to abide in Your presence, and to let Your Spirit guide my thoughts, words, and actions. I surrender my weaknesses to You and trust You to grow the fruit of self-control in my life. In Jesus' name, amen.

Devotional

Living Water: The Only Source That Truly Satisfies

Focus Scripture

John 7:37-39

"On the last and greatest day of the festival, Jesus stood and said in a loud voice, 'Let anyone who is thirsty come to me and drink. Whoever believes in me, as Scripture has said, rivers of living water will flow from within them.' By this he meant the Spirit, whom those who believed in him were later to receive."

John 4:13-14

"Jesus answered, 'Everyone who drinks this water will be thirsty again, but whoever drinks the water I give them will never thirst. Indeed, the water I give them will become in them a spring of water welling up to eternal life.'"

Introduction

I'll never forget the day I came across a video while studying for a sermon on the *Living Water*. Dr. Batmanghelidj said: *"They aren't sick—they're thirsty."* It was like a light bulb went off in my heart. He explained how people drink coffee or pop, thinking they're quenching their thirst, only to end up needing more water than before. It creates this cycle of dehydration, all because of something that *looked* like it would satisfy—but didn't.

That's exactly what the enemy does in our lives—offering things that *look* good but leave us emptier than before.

Core Message

How often do we fall for the bait? We look for fulfillment in careers, relationships, entertainment, or even destructive habits. These things *promise* satisfaction but end up draining us. The truth is, what we're really craving is only found in Jesus.

The *Living Water* He gives doesn't just satisfy for a moment—it *transforms* us. It becomes a spring inside of us, constantly pouring out purpose, peace, joy, and satisfaction.

Just like our bodies begin to crave more water when we start drinking it, our spirits crave more of Jesus when we experience the satisfaction He brings. And unlike the things of this world, *He always satisfies.*

Ways We Chase Imitations

Social Media Validation

How many times have you scrolled through your phone, posted pictures, and waited for likes or comments? For a moment, it feels good. But then, insecurity creeps in, and you're left wondering if you're enough. Only Jesus can affirm your worth in a way that lasts.

Addictions

Whether it's alcohol, drugs, or even food, we sometimes try to numb the ache in our hearts. These things might offer temporary relief, but they never heal the root of the problem. Instead, they often leave us broken and craving more. Jesus is the only one who can break those chains and give us real peace and freedom.

Relationships

We often look to people to fill the emptiness inside us— whether it's a spouse, a friend, or even our children. But no one was meant to carry that kind of weight. Only Jesus can fill the void in our hearts and give us the love we truly long for.

Career Success

We strive for promotions, titles, and recognition, thinking those things will bring purpose. But even at the top, many realize it's not enough. Jesus offers a purpose that isn't tied to our achievements but to His plans for our lives.

Entertainment and Escapism

From binge-watching TV to constant distractions, we try to escape the ache in our souls. But when the credits roll, the emptiness is still there. Jesus calls us to stop running and come to Him for true rest and fulfillment.

All these imitations look so appealing, don't they? But they'll never satisfy. What Jesus offers is different. His Living Water isn't temporary or shallow. It's not something that will leave us thirstier. It's a deep well that never runs dry—a spring that fills every empty place in our hearts.

Mind Shift

- What have you been running to for fulfillment?

- Where in your life have you been chasing imitations instead of turning to Jesus?

- How can you surrender those things and allow Him to fill your heart?

Your Mind Shift

_____

_____

_____

_____

Song Suggestion

"Fill My Cup, Lord" by CeCe Winans

This song beautifully reminds us that only Jesus can fill the empty places in our hearts. Play it as you reflect, and let its words inspire you to turn to Him for true satisfaction.

Closing Prayer

Lord, I confess that I've been looking to the wrong things to satisfy my thirst. I've chased after imitations, only to find myself more empty and tired. Forgive me for trying to fill my life with things that can never truly satisfy. Today, I come to You, the source of Living Water. Fill me with Your presence, Lord. Teach me to crave more of You every day and to trust that You will always satisfy. Thank You for offering me the eternal gift of Your Spirit. In Jesus name, Amen.

Devotional

Created to Be You (Part 1)

Focus Scripture

Ephesians 2:10 (NIV)

"For we are God's handiwork, created in Christ Jesus to do good works, which God prepared in advance for us to do."

Romans 5:2 (TLB)

"For because of our faith, he has brought us into this place of highest privilege where we now stand, and we confidently and joyfully look forward to actually becoming all that God has had in mind for us to be."

Introduction

I love thinking about how God made each of us completely unique. No two of us are exactly the same—not in our DNA, not in our fingerprints, not even in the way we laugh, think, or dream. *That blows my mind!* It's like God looked at the world and said, *"I'm going to make her special. I'm going to put a part of Me inside of her that no one else has in quite the same way."* And then He did.

But somewhere along the way, the world teaches us to *blend in.* To conform. To fit into categories and labels that were never meant for us. Instead of celebrating who God made us to be, we sometimes try to mold ourselves into what's expected, thinking that's where we'll find belonging. But have you ever noticed that the more we try to fit in, the more we lose the things that make us who we are?

Core Message

In *How Wolves Change Rivers,* a documentary about Yellowstone National Park, I learned how scientists brought wolves back after 70 years of being gone. Their absence had thrown everything off balance. The land had suffered. Without wolves to keep them in check, the deer and elk had overgrazed the land, eating so much that the trees couldn't grow, the rivers became unstable, and life started to disappear.

But when the wolves returned, they did what they were *designed* to do. And because of that, *everything changed.* Trees started growing again. Birds returned. Beavers built their dams, and even the rivers became deeper and stronger.

God created the wolves with a specific purpose. They didn't have to try to be anything other than what they were made to be, and when they walked in that purpose, *life flourished.*

And isn't that just like us?

God created each of us with a purpose. He placed something inside of us that is meant to shape the world around us. But when we try to be something we're not—when we shrink, hide, or force ourselves into places that weren't meant for us—we lose the impact we were made to have.

God didn't make you to be like everyone else. *He made you to be you.* And when you fully step into who He created you to be, *everything around you starts to shift.* You bring life. You bring balance. You bring the presence of God into places that desperately need it.

That's what it means to *joyfully and confidently* step into all that God had in mind for you to be. Not striving. Not comparing. Just *walking boldly* in the person He made you to be.

Mind Shift

- God designed me with intention—I don't have to fit into someone else's mold.

233

- When I embrace my God-given uniqueness, I help bring life and balance to the world around me.

- The way God made me is on purpose, for a purpose.

Your Mind Shift

_____

_____

_____

_____

_____

_____

Song Suggestion

" You Say " by Lauren Daigle

Closing Prayer

Father, thank You for creating me so intentionally. I don't want to waste my life trying to be someone You never designed me to be. Help me to trust that Your plan for me is good and that my uniqueness has a purpose. Show me how to walk boldly in the way You've made me. Let my life be one that brings life to the world around me, just like You intended. Amen.

Devotional

Trusting the Designer (Part 2)

Focus Scripture

Isaiah 55:8-9 (NIV)

*"For my thoughts are not your thoughts,
neither are your ways my ways," declares the
Lord. "As the heavens are higher than the
earth, so are my ways higher than your ways
and my thoughts than your thoughts."*

Proverbs 3:5-6 (NIV)

*"Trust in the Lord with all your heart and lean
not on your own understanding; in all your
ways submit to him, and he will make your
paths straight."*

Intrduction

In the last devotional, we talked about how the wolves at
Yellowstone made an incredible impact just by being who they
were created to be. But there's something else that stood out to me

in that story: *their presence didn't just restore order—it also created boundaries.*

When the wolves came back, the deer and elk couldn't just wander wherever they wanted anymore. They had to move more often, which gave trees and plants time to grow back. *Those boundaries, though inconvenient for the animals, were what allowed life to flourish again.*

And isn't that just like God's ways?

His design includes boundaries. His order of things may sometimes seem inconvenient or even outdated, but we don't have to understand—we just need to trust Him.

Core Message

There are times when God's ways don't make sense to me. I like to have a plan, to see where I'm going, to know why things happen the way they do. But following God doesn't always come with explanations. Sometimes, He simply asks me to trust Him, even when I don't understand.

The wolves at Yellowstone didn't have to understand the science behind the changes they caused. *They just had to be wolves.* And we don't have to understand everything about God's ways—we just have to obey.

And when we do, we will be amazed at the beauty, depth, and strength that begins to grow in our lives. The surprises will come— not because we controlled the outcome, but because we *let the Designer do what only He can do.*

Mind Shift

- God's ways are higher than mine—I don't have to understand everything to trust Him.

- Obedience brings blessings I may not see right away.

- Boundaries are not meant to hold me back, but to bring life and growth.

- God is the Designer. He knows what He's doing, and I can trust Him.

Your Mind Shift:

_____

_____

_____

_____

_____

_____

_____

Song Suggestion

"Trust in You" by Lauren Daigle

Closing Prayer

Father, there are so many times I don't understand what You're doing. Sometimes Your ways seem hard or confusing, and I struggle to trust. But I know that You are the Designer. You see the whole picture when I only see a tiny part. Help me to obey You even when I don't understand. Help me to trust that Your boundaries are for my good and that following You leads to life. Thank You for knowing what I need, even when I don't. Amen.

Day 55

Growing Your Roots

1. Faithfulness, My Steady Anchor: 2 Timothy 2: 13 If we are faithless, He remains faithful, for He cannot disown Himself.

Your Mind Shift

_____

_____

_____

_____

2. Self-Control: Saying No to Say Yes: Daniel 1:8 But Daniel resolved not to defile himself with the royal food and wine, and he asked the chief official for permission not to defile himself this way.

Your Mind Shift

_____

_____

_____

_____

3. Living Water, the Only Source That Truely Satisfies: John
    4:13-14 *"Jesus answered, 'Everyone who drinks this water
    will be thirsty again, but whoever drinks the water I give them
    will never thirst. Indeed, the water I give them will become in
    them a spring of water welling up to eternal life.'"*

Your Mind Shift

_____

_____

_____

_____

4. Created To Be You (Part 1): Ephesians 2:10 (NIV) – *"For we
    are God's handiwork, created in Christ Jesus to do good
    works, which God prepared in advance for us to do."*

Romans 5:2 (TLB) – *"For because of our faith, he has brought us
into this place of highest privilege where we now stand, and we
confidently and joyfully look forward to actually becoming all that
God has had in mind for us to be."*

Your Mind Shift

_____

_____

_____

_____

5. Created To Be You (Part 2): Isaiah 55:8-9 (NIV) – *"For my thoughts are not your thoughts, neither are your ways my ways," declares the Lord. "As the heavens are higher than the earth, so are my ways higher than your ways and my thoughts than your thoughts."*

Proverbs 3:5-6 (NIV) – *"Trust in the Lord with all your heart and lean not on your own understanding; in all your ways submit to him, and he will make your paths straight."*

Your Mind Shift

_____

_____

_____

_____

Which of these do you feel the Holy Spirit leading you to focus on today? You can also look back at other Mind Shift Days and see if the Holy Spirit draws you to any of them. He knows your heart. He also knows the week that you have had and the one you have coming. Seek Him. Write below any new mind shifts that you need to remember or any new insights.

_____

_____

_____

_____

Closing Prayer

Lord, You are faithful and true. You are the One that I can always depend on. Thank You for that. Help me become the me that You created me to be. And please help me to give myself grace in the process. I am Your handiwork. I am on Your mind. I can trust You to take my imperfect self and use me for Your glory. I want to be more and more like You Lord. Thank You for never giving up on me and always encouraging me. In Jesus Name, Amen.

Day 56

Finishing the Week In Worship

Another week to be grateful. Today I would like you to ask God to show you more of who you are. The unique way that you represent Him to the world. He didn't make a mistake. You are a work of art from the same Hands that make every sunset and mountain.

Write down what God shows you.

_____

_____

_____

_____

_____

_____

_____

If you are struggling with that, here are some examples: I'm still trying. I'm kind. I like elderly people. I love to sing. I organize. I go with the flow. I lead. I'm a good team player. ETC

Closing Prayer

Lord thank You for giving me life. Thank You for saving me from myself. Thank You for believing in me and seeking me when I was such a mess. Thank You for not giving up on me when I gave up on You. Lord I am fearfully and wonderfully made. I believe You. I'm gonna learn to love me too, like You do. I ask You to please keep pouring Your love into me. I know that with You in me, I can do anything. In Jesus Name, Amen.

Devotional

Taking Control of Your Mind

Focus Scripture

---

2 Corinthians 10:5

"We demolish arguments and every pretension that sets itself up against the knowledge of God, and we take captive every thought to make it obedient to Christ."

Introduction

Do you ever feel like your mind is running the show? *I've been there.* One negative thought turns into a spiral of doubts, fears, and *what ifs* that pull me away from peace. It's overwhelming, and it's exactly why *2 Corinthians 10:5* is so important.

Core Message

It says we *demolish* arguments and *take captive* every thought to make it obedient to Christ. Those words—*demolish* and *take* captive—tell us this is a battle. *It's not passive; it's intentional.* But here's the key: this isn't a battle we can win on our own. No amount of determination or self-talk will make those thoughts submit. *We need the Holy Spirit working in us.*

That's the difference-maker. God's power—the same power that raised Jesus from the dead—is alive in us. *With Him, we can tear down lies and replace them with truth.*

Here's what it looks like in real life:

If I start feeling like *I'm not enough*, I have to stop that thought and replace it with what God says. His Word reminds me that being *poor in spirit*—knowing I need Him—is exactly where I need to be.

Or when I catch myself assuming someone's social media post is about me, I stop. *That's just my imagination running wild.* I don't need to fight battles that don't exist.

Those thoughts don't have to control us, but *we have to take action.* It's not enough to ignore them; we need to confront them with God's truth and intentionally shift our focus.

Our minds are like well-worn paths. Old thought patterns are easy to fall into because they're familiar. Creating new ones takes effort. Imagine clearing a trail in a dense forest. It's hard work at first, but with time, the path becomes clear.

The Holy Spirit is the one who helps us clear that path. When a negative thought pops up, I've learned to stop and replace it with something true. Sometimes it's a scripture I've memorized. Other times it's a simple, *Thank You, Jesus, for dying for me.*

Here's another way to think about it: A bird may land on your head, but you don't have to let it build a nest. When those thoughts pop up, you don't have to let them settle in and take over. Stop them, replace them with truth, and move forward.

And don't wait until the heat of the moment—prepare ahead of time. Write down scriptures, keep a worship song in your heart, or think of a simple phrase to redirect your mind. With God's help, you can train your mind to think differently.

Mind Shift

Take a moment to reflect and write down your thoughts:

- What negative thoughts have been taking control of your mind lately?

- What truth from God's Word can you use to replace those thoughts? Write it down and keep it somewhere you can see it.

- How can you invite the Holy Spirit into your thought life today?

Your Mind Shift

_____

_____

_____

_____

Song Suggestion

"Losing My Mind" by Tory G

This song beautifully captures the struggle of the mind and the victory we have in Christ. Let it inspire you to trust God in the battle for your thoughts and do something different!

Closing Prayer

Lord, You see the thoughts that try to pull me away from Your truth. I confess that I've let some of those thoughts take control, but today I choose to stop them and make them obedient to Christ. Holy Spirit, I need Your help. Remind me of the truth in Your Word and give me the strength to demolish the lies. Thank You for the resurrection power that lives in me and for the victory I have in You. In Jesus' name, Amen.

Devotional

Sacrifice of Atonement

Focus Scripture

Romans 3:25a (NIV)

"God presented Christ as a sacrifice of atonement, through the shedding of his blood— to be received by faith."

Introduction

Salvation is such a beautiful gift, and I love how the Bible connects everything together to help us understand what Jesus has done for us. To fully grasp the depth of this gift, we need to start with what God established in the Old Testament.

Core Message

When the Israelites carried the Tabernacle through the wilderness, at the very center of it was the *Holy of Holies*. Inside the *Holy of Holies* was the *Ark of the Covenant*, and its lid was called the *mercy seat*. This wasn't just a sacred object—it was the place where God's presence dwelled *above the mercy seat*. However, only the high priest could enter the *Holy of Holies*, and only *once a year* on the *Day of Atonement*. On that day, the high priest would sprinkle the blood of a spotless animal on the *mercy seat* to atone for the sins of the people.

This act of sacrifice was a *shadow* of what was to come. Hebrews 9:12 tells us:

"He (Jesus) did not enter by means of the blood of goats and calves; but he entered the Most Holy Place once for all by his own blood, thus obtaining eternal redemption."

Jesus offered His own blood as the ultimate *sacrifice of atonement*—not to cover sins *temporarily* like the animal sacrifices, but to cleanse us *completely and eternally*. His blood was applied not to a physical *mercy seat* in the Tabernacle, but to the hearts of those who believe in Him.

Here's what makes this even more beautiful: just as God's presence dwelled *above the mercy seat* in the *Holy of Holies*, now His presence *dwells within us*. Ephesians 3:17 says,

"So that Christ may dwell in your hearts through faith."

The place where the blood was applied in the Old Testament was where God's presence rested. And now, *where the blood of Jesus is applied to our hearts through faith, He dwells within us.*

Think about that. The same God who commanded the Israelites to construct the *Tabernacle* so He could dwell *among* them now chooses to dwell *within* His people. Through the sacrifice of Jesus, we have *direct access to God*—not just *once a year,* not through a high priest, but *every day, in every moment,* because His Spirit lives within us.

If you've never invited Jesus into your heart, know this: *He has already paid the price for your sins.* His blood was shed to bring you *forgiveness, freedom,* and the *incredible gift* of His presence dwelling in you now and living with Him for eternity in Heaven one day. By faith, you can receive Him as your Savior, trusting in His *sacrifice of atonement* for your sins.

Mind Shift

- ☐ Take time to reflect on this powerful truth: *the God whose presence dwelled above the Ark of the Covenant in the Holy of Holies now chooses to dwell within you.*

- ☐ How does this understanding impact your view of *salvation, forgiveness,* and your *relationship with Him?*

Your Mind Shift

_____

_____

_____

_____

Song Suggestion

"Jesus Paid It All" – This song beautifully reminds us of the eternal price Jesus paid for our sins. Reflect on the words and thank Him for the gift of salvation.

Closing Prayer

Father, thank You for sending Jesus as the perfect sacrifice of atonement. Thank You that His blood doesn't just cover my sins temporarily but cleanses me completely. I am in awe that You now choose to dwell within me. Help me to live in a way that honors this incredible truth. For anyone who doesn't yet know You, I ask that You soften their hearts and draw them to You. Thank You for Your mercy, Your love, and the eternal redemption You offer through Jesus. In His Jesus name. Amen

Devotional

Abiding in the Tabernacle of His Presence

Focus Scripture

John 15:4

"Remain in me, as I also remain in you. No branch can bear fruit by itself; it must remain in the vine. Neither can you bear fruit unless you remain in me."

Exodus 25:8

"Then have them make a sanctuary for me, and I will dwell among them."

Introduction

God *wants* to dwell with us. Let that sink in for a moment. The *Creator of the universe*, the One who *holds the stars in place* and *causes the sun to rise*, desires to be with *you* and *me*. This truth has changed my life, and I hope it will change yours too.

Core Message

In the *Old Testament*, God commanded the Israelites to build a tabernacle—a sacred space where His presence would dwell among His people. The word *tabernacle* means to dwell or take up residence. *Imagine that.* The *holy* God who *parted the Red Sea* and *provided manna from heaven* wanted to take up residence with His people.

It wasn't about *grandeur* or *performance*—it was about relationship. *God wanted to be near them.*

Fast forward to the *New Testament*, and we see this desire take on a new form. In *John 15*, Jesus invites us to abide in Him. The word *abide* means to dwell, to stay, to live in Him. Jesus describes Himself as the true vine, and we are the branches. He says we *cannot do anything* apart from Him.

This picture of *abiding* is one of intimacy, dependence, and connection. It's not about striving—it's about staying. It's about *planting ourselves in His presence* and *drawing nourishment from Him.*

The connection between the *tabernacle* and *abiding* is profound. In the *Old Testament*, God's presence dwelled in a temporary, physical space. In the *New Testament*, through Jesus, that dwelling becomes internal.

The *same* God who once dwelled in the tabernacle now dwells in us through His Spirit.

We are invited to *take off our shoes*, *get cozy*, and *rest in Him*—not just *occasionally*, but every day.

Practicing His Presence

I recently revisited *Practicing the Presence of God* by Brother Lawrence, and it reminded me of the simplicity and beauty of *abiding* in God. Brother Lawrence, a monk in a monastery, learned to carry God's presence with him throughout his day. Whether he was scrubbing pots or in prayer, he made a *conscious effort* to be aware of God with him.

I've tried to implement this practice in my own life. Over the years, I've done small things to remind myself to stay connected to Him. I've set alarms on my phone to pause and acknowledge His presence. I've changed my screensaver to reflect a scripture I'm meditating on. I've painted one fingernail a different color or put a rock in my pocket—*simple, tangible reminders that He is with me.*

This isn't about creating *more work* for ourselves. It's about *inviting God* into the *mundane moments* of our lives. Whether we're folding laundry, driving to work, or sitting in silence—*He is there.*

The more aware we become of *His presence,* the more we'll *know Him and His love.*

Fruitfulness Comes from Connection

Jesus said, "Apart from Me, you can do nothing." That's a sobering statement. All of our striving, planning, and working amounts to nothing if we're not connected to Him. But the opposite is also true—when we stay connected to the true vine, we will bear fruit. And this fruit isn't just for show; it's evidence of His life flowing through us.

Think about a branch on a grapevine. It doesn't have to work to produce grapes. Its job is simply to stay connected to the vine, where it receives the nutrients it needs. In the same way, our job is to stay connected to Jesus. The fruit—love, joy, peace, patience, kindness, goodness, faithfulness, gentleness, and self-control—will naturally come as a result of abiding in Him.

The tabernacle was a place where God's people could experience His presence and glory. Today, we don't have to travel to a physical place to meet with Him. He has made His home in us. When we remain in Him, we'll find that He is our source of life, our strength, and our joy.

A Relationship, Not a Checklist

One of the most freeing truths I've learned is that *abiding in Christ is not about performance—it's about presence.* God isn't asking us to check off a list of spiritual tasks. *He's inviting us into a relationship.* He wants to *nourish our souls, guide our steps, and fill our lives with His love.*

Fifteen years ago, I began to *practice this truth* in small ways, and it has *transformed* my relationship with God. Some days, I do it well; other days, I fall short. *But His grace meets me every time.*

He is *patient* with us as we *learn to abide in Him.* He doesn't demand *perfection*—just a *willing heart.*

Mind Shift

Take a moment to reflect on this truth: God wants to dwell with you. Not because of what you've done but because of who He is. He loves you and desires to walk with you through every moment of your day.

What can you do this week to remind yourself of His presence? Maybe it's setting an alarm, placing a sticky note on your mirror, or starting your day with a simple prayer: "Lord, help me abide in You today." These small steps can make a big difference in cultivating a life of abiding. It's not about performance; its about presence.

Your Mind Shift

_____

_____

_____

_____

Song Suggestion

Abide with Me by Matt Maher

Closing Prayer

As we begin this journey of exploring the tabernacle and abiding, remember this: God's ultimate goal is relationship. He wants to be with you. Let that truth shape your week and draw you closer to Him.

Devotional

Don't Forget What You Look Like

Focus Scripture

James 1:23-24

"Anyone who listens to the Word but does not do what it says is like a man who looks at his face in the mirror and, after looking at himself, goes away and immediately forgets what he looks like."

Introduction

I was so frustrated. My child had just done the *exact* thing I told them not to do—for the third time. I had *warned, explained,* and even *threatened a consequence*, and yet, here we were. *Again.* I felt the irritation rise in my chest as I started to lecture, but in the middle of my words, I had one of those moments where *God holds up a mirror to my own heart.*

How many times have *I* done the very thing *God* has told me *not* to do? How often have I *read His Word, felt conviction, and promised to change—only to find myself repeating the same sin?* Just like my child in front of me, *I have ignored warnings. I have resisted wisdom. I have chosen my own way even when I knew better.*

And yet, *God's response to me is not exasperation. It's mercy.*

Core Message

Inside the *tabernacle*, the Israelites had to go through a process every time they made a *sacrifice*. They couldn't just bring the animal and be done with it. No, the sacrifice was *messy—literally*. They would end up with *blood on their hands, their clothes, even their faces*. And then, after the sacrifice was made, they had to go to the *water basin* to wash.

I can only imagine the moment they leaned over that water and saw their own reflection—*streaks of blood reminding them that a life had been given*. It was a *visual reminder* of both *the cost of sin* and *the gift of cleansing*.

This is exactly what *James 1:23-24* warns us about:

"Anyone who listens to the word but does not do what it says is like someone who looks at his face in a mirror and, after looking at himself, goes away and immediately forgets what he looks like."

We are *not* meant to *glance* at the truth of our condition and then walk away *as if nothing has changed.* We are meant to remember.

To remember our need for a *Savior.*

To remember the *sacrifice* that was made for us.

To remember that we are *no better—and no worse—than anyone else.*

When I looked at my child that day, I had a choice. I could let frustration win and *shame* them for their disobedience, or I could let that *mirror moment* shape my response. Yes, *correction was needed,* but *what if I corrected with the same patience and love God has given me?*

What if, instead of reacting in *frustration,* I led with *compassion?*

That's what God calls us to do—not to *ignore sin,* but to see *our own need for grace* so clearly that we extend it to others. Being confronted with our *faults* isn't meant to bring *condemnation,* but *humility.* When we see our own struggles, it should grow *compassion* in us, not *self-righteousness or shame.*

The reality is, *we all need the blood of Jesus.* That's the *only* thing that washes us *clean.*

Nothing we do makes us *more worthy* of salvation than someone else. And *nothing we've done* makes us *beyond saving.*

Either *we've been washed in the blood of Christ, or we haven't. That's it.*

So let's *not* forget what we look like. Let's *not* forget *where we've come from*, or *how much we've been forgiven.*

And let's allow that remembrance to shape *how we love those around us*—especially in the moments when *frustration* tries to take over.

Mind Shift

Take a moment to reflect on a time when you've been frustrated with someone else's actions. How might your response have been different if you had remembered your own need for grace in that moment? Ask God to help you see others through the lens of His mercy, just as He sees you.

Your Mind Shift

_____

_____

_____

_____

_____

_____

Song Suggestion

Mercy said NO by CeCe Winan

Closing Prayer

Father, thank You for the sacrifice of Jesus. Thank You for loving me enough to wash me clean when I could never do it myself. Help me to remember who I am apart from Your grace so that I never look down on someone else. When I see my own sin, let it humble me, not condemn me. And when I see the struggles of others, let me respond with the same patience, kindness, and love that You have shown me. May I never forget what I look like in light of Your mercy. In Jesus' name, Amen.

Devotional

The Lampstand: A Life Shaped by God's Hands

Focus Scripture

Matthew 5:16

In the same way, let your light shine before others, so that they may see your good works and give glory to your Father who is in Heaven.

Introduction

When I think about the lampstand in the tabernacle, I am struck by how detailed God's instructions were for its creation. It wasn't just any piece of furniture; it was to be crafted from pure gold, hammered from a single solid piece. Not molded, not pieced together, but hammered out. That detail matters.

I imagine the hammering process—each strike shaping, refining, bringing out the beauty hidden within the gold. It reminds me of the way Michelangelo described sculpting. He saw a masterpiece inside the stone and simply had to remove what didn't belong to reveal what was already there. That's exactly how God works with us. He sees the person we were created to be, but sometimes, the shaping requires a hammer and a chisel. It isn't always easy, but it is always purposeful.

Core Message

The lampstand wasn't just about being beautiful; it had a function. It was the only source of light in the tabernacle. Without it, the holy place would be in complete darkness. The light didn't come from the gold itself, but from the oil flowing through it, fueling the flame. Without the oil, it would just be a beautifully crafted piece of gold sitting in the dark.

The oil represents the Holy Spirit. Without Him, we have no light. We can be refined, shaped, and even look the part, but without the Spirit of God flowing through us, we remain in darkness. This is why the hammering matters. It isn't just about looking good on the outside; it's about becoming a vessel that carries His presence, a lamp that actually shines.

The Symbolism of Almonds

The lampstand was not only shaped with precision, but it was also decorated with almond flowers and buds. Almonds are significant in Scripture because they symbolize resurrection life. In Numbers 17, Aaron's rod, which had been just a dead stick, budded, blossomed, and produced almonds overnight. It was a sign of God's chosen and an undeniable display of His power to bring life where there was none.

The connection is clear. The lampstand, designed to give light, was covered in symbols of resurrection. This is a picture of our own spiritual lives. When we allow God to shape us, when we die to ourselves, His resurrected life flows through us, and the light within us shines for others to see.

We are the tabernacle now. If we have surrendered our lives to Christ and accepted His sacrifice on the cross, then His Spirit resides in us. We are the lampstand. The question is, are we allowing His light to shine?

A Work in Progress

Philippians 1:6 comes to mind:

"Being confident of this, that He who began a good work in you will carry it on to completion until the day of Christ Jesus."

The process of being hammered out, refined, and filled with His Spirit is ongoing. Sometimes, it feels like we are being pounded from every side. Life can be painful. Trials can be overwhelming. But God is at work. Every challenge, every difficulty is another strike of the hammer, shaping us into who we were always meant to be.

When we yield to Him, when we stop resisting and start trusting, the oil flows, the light ignites, and our lives become a beacon for those still lost in the darkness.

Mind Shift

- I am being shaped with purpose, not punished without reason.

- The Holy Spirit is my source of light—I cannot shine on my own.

- As I surrender, God's resurrected life flows through me.

- He who began a good work in me will be faithful to complete it.

Your Mind Shift

_____

_____

_____

_____

_____

_____

Song Suggestion

"Go Light Your World" by Kathy Troccoli

This song is a perfect reminder that we are called to carry the light of Christ into the world. It isn't about us; it's about the Spirit within us. So, let Him shape you. Let Him refine you. Let His light shine through you.

Closing Prayer

Lord, I surrender to Your refining work in my life. I know that sometimes the hammering hurts, but I trust that You are shaping me into something beautiful, something that reflects Your glory. Fill me with Your Spirit, Lord. Let Your oil flow through me so that my life is not just a crafted vessel, but a shining light. When I feel weary, remind me that You are still at work, and that You will complete what You have started in me. Let Your resurrected life flow through me, and may my light shine so that others see You. In Jesus' name, Amen.

Day 62

Growing Your Roots

Lord, as I look at the mind shifts that You have shown me these last five days, draw my attention to the seeds in my heart that need to be fed. Show me the Truth again and give me the courage to pull out the lies that are choking my faith. In Jesus Name. Amen.

1. Taking Control of Your Mind: 2 Corinthians 10:5 *"We demolish arguments and every pretension that sets itself up against the knowledge of God, and we take captive every thought to make it obedient to Christ."*

Your Mind Shift

_____

_____

_____

_____

2. Sacrifice of Atonement: Romans 3:25a "God presented Christ as a sacrifice of atonement, through the shedding of his blood—to be received by faith." – Romans 3:25a (NIV)

Your Mind Shift

_____

_____

_____

_____

3. Abiding in the Tabernacle of His Presence: John 15:4 "Remain in me, as I also remain in you. No branch can bear fruit by itself; it must remain in the vine. Neither can you bear fruit unless you remain in me." Exodus 25:8 Then have them make a sanctuary for me, and I will dwell among them.

Your Mind Shift

_____

_____

_____

_____

4. Don't Forget What You Look Like: *James 1:23-24* Anyone who listens to the Word but does not do what it says is like a man who looks at his face in the mirror and after looking at himself goes away and immediately forgets what he looks like.

Your Mind Shift

_____

_____

_____

_____

5. The Lampstand; A Life Shaped By God: Focus Scripture: Matthew 5:16 In the same way, let your light shine before others, so that they may see your good works and give glory to your Father who is in Heaven.

Your Mind Shift

_____

_____

_____

_____

Reread the devotional/s that you feel the Holy Spirit drawing you to. Write below any new mind shifts that God has shown you.

_____

_____

_____

_____

_____

Closing Prayer

Holy Spirit thank You for the way You show up for me every day. Keep the soil of my heart ready for Truth to be planted and quick to take out a lie that is trying to take root in my heart and mind. Keep doing this new thing in me. In Jesus Name. Amen.

Day 63

Finishing the Week In Worship

Today I would like you to pray the prayer below and then skim over your Mind Shifts beginning with Day 6 and remind yourself of what God has been teaching you. You don't need to go over all of them, but stop where the Holy Spirit leads you to. Then write that Mind Shift down and answer the questions below.

Your Mind Shift

_____

_____

_____

_____

Has this Mind Shift taken root in your life? What is the evidence?

_____

_____

_____

_____

Is there a scripture that you need to memorize that will help feed this Mind Shift? Or a song that you need to keep on the top of your playlist this week? Ask the Lord to show you what will remind you of this new Truth so that the birds don't come and snatch it up.

_____

_____

_____

_____

Listen to one of the songs that draw you close to the Lord.

Closing Prayer

Lord first I just want to say thank You for loving me on this journey and never giving up on me. I ask You to please keep my heart hungry for You and Your Presence. And this Mind Shift that You have brought to my mind today, plant it deep within me. Help me to enjoy conviction and repentance that leads me to the freedom I seek. The Truth sets me free. I believe you. In Jesus Name, Amen.

Devotional

Blessed Are the Poor in Spirit: The Foundation of Faith

Focus Scripture

Matthew 5:3

"Blessed are the poor in spirit, for theirs is the kingdom of heaven."

Introduction

The *Beatitudes* represent the beginning of our relationship with Christ and the journey of growth that follows. They outline what it looks like to live in a position of blessing—a state of *spiritual well-being, joy, and favor* that comes from being in *right relationship* with God.

Core Message

The word "blessed", as used in the New Testament, is rich with meaning. In Greek, it's *makarios*, which describes a deep, abiding joy and contentment. This joy isn't tied to our *circumstances* but flows from the grace and favor of God. Being blessed is a position of receiving from Him—a position that begins with *recognizing our spiritual poverty*.

Jesus said, *"Blessed are the poor in spirit."* This is where it all starts. To be *"poor in spirit"* is to recognize that, *spiritually, we have nothing to offer.* On our own, we are bankrupt.

But instead of being a place of shame, this is a *beautiful starting point*.

It's in realizing our need that we open ourselves to receive from God.

A Beautiful Place to Be

Admitting that we are *poor in spirit* doesn't come naturally. We live in a culture that *celebrates independence and strength*, yet the reality is, we can't even make our hearts beat once on our own. Still, we resist admitting our need.

For some, being *poor in spirit* happens when they reach the end of themselves. Think of someone who has *hit rock bottom*—whether through *addiction, heartbreak, or failure*. They've *tried everything else*, and it hasn't worked. In that moment of surrender, when they *cry out for help*, they discover God's grace waiting to meet them.

For others, it might be about letting go of self-righteousness. Maybe you've felt like being *"good enough"* or *doing all the right things* would *earn you favor with God*. But true righteousness can't be earned. It's only when we let go of our efforts and *rely on Jesus' finished work on the cross* that we experience freedom.

And then there's the daily dependence that comes with *walking with God*. From the *air we breathe* to the *strength we need to get through each day*, every moment of our lives is sustained by Him. Recognizing that dependence is part of *living as someone who is poor in spirit.*

Until I recognize my need, the *Savior* is of no use to me.

If I don't see that I'm drowning, I won't reach for the lifeboat.

If I don't acknowledge that I'm lost, I won't ask for directions.

It's when I understand my need for Jesus that He becomes my everything.

This is the beginning of faith—a *relationship built not on what we bring to the table, but on what Jesus has already done for us.*

Mind Shift

Take some time to reflect and write down your thoughts:

- Where in your life have you been striving to do it all on your own? Maybe it's in trying to break a bad habit, prove your worth, or carry a burden that feels too heavy.

- How can you admit your need for God in a deeper way?

- What would it look like to fully depend on Him instead of your own strength?

Your Mind Shift

_____

_____

_____

_____

Song Suggestion

"Lord, I Need You" by Matt Maher

This song is a powerful reminder of our constant need for God's presence, grace, and strength. Let the words guide you into a posture of surrender and worship.

Closing Prayer

Lord, I confess that I've tried to do so much on my own. I've tried to be strong, independent, and self-sufficient, but I know now that I can't do this life without You. I am poor in spirit, Lord. I have nothing to offer and everything to receive. Thank You for Your grace and favor that meet me in my need. Help me to live in complete dependence on You, trusting in Your righteousness and not my own. Teach me to embrace my need as a beautiful place where Your blessings flow. In Jesus' name, Amen.

Devotional

Blessed Are Those Who Mourn

Focus Scripture

Matthew 5:4 (ESV)

"Blessed are those who mourn, for they shall be comforted."

Introduction

When we hear the word *mourn*, our minds often go to grief over losing a loved one. That is a *very real and deep* kind of mourning, but Jesus is pointing to something else in this verse. He's talking about mourning over sin—*our sin*, the *weight of it*, and the separation it creates between us and God.

Core Message

The first beatitude teaches us to recognize our spiritual bankruptcy—that we are *completely incapable of saving ourselves.*

The second beatitude takes it further: *once we recognize our sin, we should feel the weight of it and mourn over it.* But not in a way that leads to shame or hopelessness—in a way that brings us to true repentance.

There's a big difference between *being sorry* and *being repentant.* Saying *"I'm sorry"* because we *got caught* or *don't like the consequences* of our actions isn't the same as being heartbroken over how our sin grieves the heart of God.

I once heard someone say, *"I'm sorry without changed behavior is manipulation."*

How many times have we said *sorry* just to smooth things over, with no real intention of changing?

God is not fooled by *empty apologies.* He knows our hearts. He *sees beyond our tears and sad expressions.* He knows whether we truly desire to *turn away from sin* or if we just want to escape the discomfort of conviction.

Real mourning over sin leads to a change of heart and a change of direction.

That's what repentance is—it's not just feeling bad, it's *turning around and going the other way.*

And when we do that, something beautiful happens:

We are comforted.

Comfort That Heals

The comfort Jesus speaks of here isn't just a pat on the back or a temporary relief. The word for *comforted* in the original language means to *come alongside*, to *encourage*, to *rally someone forward*. It's a word that's also used to describe the Holy Spirit—our Advocate, our Helper.

When we truly grieve over our sin and turn to God, He doesn't leave us to sit in despair. He comes alongside us. He encourages us. He reminds us of His forgiveness and leads us toward healing and restoration.

And He doesn't just do this through His Spirit—He also uses people. Our brothers and sisters in Christ are part of this comfort. When we confess our struggles, when we bring our sin into the light instead of hiding in shame, we find strength and encouragement in the body of Christ. There is power in vulnerability. There is freedom in confession. James 5:16 Confess therefore your sins one to another, and pray one for another, that you may be healed.

The enemy wants us to believe that our sin makes us unworthy of God's love. That if people knew the real us, they would turn away.

But the truth is, we all fall short. And the comfort of God meets us right in the middle of our brokenness.

Mind Shift

1. Do I grieve over my sin, or do I just dislike the consequences of it?

2. Am I truly repentant, or do I try to manipulate God and others with surface-level apologies?

3. Have I experienced the comfort of God in my repentance?

4. Who in my life can I be open with about my struggles, so I don't battle sin alone?

Take a moment to write down your thoughts. Be honest with yourself and with God.

Your Mind Shift

_____

_____

_____

_____

_____

Song Suggestion

"Give Me a Clean Heart" by Margaret Douroux

Closing Prayer

Father, I don't want to just be sorry—I want to be changed. I don't want to manipulate my way out of consequences. I want to truly mourn over my sin because I know it grieves Your heart. I ask for Your forgiveness and for the strength to turn away from anything that separates me from You. Thank You for Your comfort, for the way You don't leave me in my brokenness but walk with me into healing. Help me to be honest about my struggles and surround myself with people who will encourage me in righteousness. In Jesus' name, Amen.

Short Quote

"True repentance is not just a feeling of regret, but a change of heart that leads to a change of direction." — Unknown

Devotional

Blessed Are the Meek

Focus Scripture

Matthew 5:5

"Blessed are the meek, for they shall inherit the earth."

Introduction

We have been on a journey of learning what it truly means to follow Jesus. First, we recognized our deep need for Him—we were spiritually poor, utterly incapable of saving ourselves. Then, as we saw our sin for what it really was, we mourned. But in that mourning, we found a God who didn't leave us in our sorrow. He comforted us, lifted our heads, and surrounded us with His love and His people.

Core Message

Now, we are learning obedience. Not perfectly—far from it. But we are growing. Our hearts are softening. We don't always get it right, but our desire is to do things God's way. Philippians 3:13-14 reminds us that we press on, leaving behind our old ways and straining toward what lies ahead. We've done it our way before, and we know where that leads. But now, our hearts are inclined toward the Lord. We want to please Him.

This is where meekness comes in.

When I think of meekness, I think of being pliable—willing to be shaped and molded by God. It's the opposite of being stiff-necked, like the Israelites who constantly resisted Him. Ezekiel 36:26 says that God has removed our heart of stone and given us a heart of flesh. A heart that listens. A heart that yields. A heart that desires His way more than our own.

Meekness is not weakness. It's not passivity. It's not being walked over. It is power under control. It is a heart that submits to God even when the flesh wants to rise up. It is choosing humility when pride wants to take over. It is responding with gentleness when anger feels more satisfying.

The world tells us to push back, to fight for our way, to demand our rights. But Jesus tells us something completely different. He says that the meek—the ones who yield, who trust, who don't force their own way—are the ones who inherit the earth. Not just a piece of land, not just a moment of success, but the eternal Kingdom of God.

This characteristic of meekness is also a fruit of the Spirit (Galatians 5:22-23). It is a mark of a child of God. When you walk in meekness, the evidence of His Spirit in you becomes clear. The world may not understand it, but heaven rejoices.

So, how do we walk in meekness?

We stay attentive to His voice. We yield. We surrender. We let His Word transform us. And when we fail, we get back up, ask for His help, and keep walking in obedience.

The meek will inherit the earth. What a promise. What a calling.

Let's keep learning to be pliable in His hands.

Mind Shift

What has the Holy Spirit shown you about meekness? How is He calling you to surrender and yield more fully to Him?

Your Mind Shift

_____

_____

_____

_____

_____

_____

Song Suggestion

"We Fall Down" by Donnie McClurkin

Closing Prayer

Father,

I come before You, aware that my heart still wrestles with pride and self-will. I don't want to be stiff-necked like the Israelites—I want to be pliable, teachable, and fully surrendered to You. Thank You for softening my heart, for removing my heart of stone, and for giving me a heart of flesh.

Help me to walk in meekness, to yield to Your Spirit, and to trust that Your way is always better than mine. When I fail, remind me of Your grace and gently lead me back to You.

I desire to inherit all that You have for me, Lord.

In Jesus' name, Amen.

Devotional

Hungry and Thirsty

Focus Scripture

Matthew 5:6

"Blessed are those who hunger and thirst for righteousness, for they shall be filled."

Introduction

I can't tell you how much I love the coconut cream donut from Tim Hortons. That creamy, coconutty goodness is something I crave. The other day, I went to pick one up, and they were out. So I stopped at another location, and they were also out. Determined, I called a third Tim Hortons, and guess what? No coconut cream donuts there either.

At this point, I was on a mission. The next morning, I made sure to go early, and persistence paid off—I finally got my donut. And let me tell you, that first bite was everything I had been craving.

That kind of craving—the kind that puts you into action, that makes you go out of your way until you're satisfied—is exactly what Jesus was talking about in Matthew 5:6.

Core Message

When Jesus says, "Blessed are those who hunger and thirst for righteousness," He's talking about an earnest craving, an unshakable desire to be right with God. It's not just a casual interest or a "would-be-nice" thought—it's a deep, driving hunger, like the one that had me checking multiple Tim Hortons for a donut. But instead of something sweet and temporary, this craving leads to something eternally satisfying.

So what exactly are we craving when we hunger and thirst for righteousness? We are craving rightness with God. We are longing for His approval, to be declared righteous before Him. But here's the thing—how do we get that?

Romans 4:25 tells us, "He was delivered over to death for our sins and was raised to life for our justification." That word justification is huge. It means to be declared righteous, to be exonerated. Jesus was handed over to die because of our sins, and He was raised back to life so that we could be made right with God.

Romans 5:1-2 makes it even clearer:

"Therefore, since we have been justified through faith, we have peace with God through our Lord Jesus Christ, through whom we have gained access by faith into this grace in which we now stand."

This means that our rightness with God doesn't come from our own efforts. It comes through faith in Jesus—faith in His sacrifice, His resurrection, and His love for us. It is faith that declares us righteous.

So if we are truly hungry and thirsty for righteousness, what we are really craving is more faith. More belief in Him. More trust in His ways. More assurance that He is for us, that He loves us, and that He alone satisfies.

That kind of hunger leads to action. Just like my relentless pursuit of that coconut cream donut, a heart that longs for righteousness will go out of its way to seek God. It will press in through prayer, through His Word, through worship, and through obedience. And Jesus promises that when we seek Him this way, we will be filled.

This is not an empty hunger. This is not a thirst that will leave us dry. It is a craving that God delights in satisfying.

Augustine once said, "You have made us for yourself, O Lord, and our heart is restless until it rests in you."

We were created to crave God. The more we pursue Him, the more we will be filled.

Mind Shift

- My hunger and thirst for righteousness is a craving for more of God, not more of religion.

- Righteousness is not something I earn—it's something I receive through faith in Jesus.

- If I truly desire righteousness, my life will reflect that desire in how I seek God daily.

- God promises to satisfy my hunger for Him when I pursue Him with my whole heart.

Your Mind Shift

_____

_____

_____

_____

_____

_____

Song

Nothing Else – Cody Carnes

Closing Prayer

Lord, I want to crave You more. I don't want to be satisfied with anything less than Your righteousness. Stir up a deep hunger and thirst in me to know You, to seek You, and to believe You more. Fill me as I chase after You.

Devotional

Blessed Are the Merciful

Focus Scripture

Matthew 5:7

*"Blessed are the merciful, for they will be
shown mercy."*

Introduction

The Beatitudes take us on a journey of spiritual growth. We begin by recognizing our deep need for a Savior, then mourn over our sin and repent, turning our hearts toward God. We learn to be meek, yielding our will to His. As we mature, we hunger and thirst for righteousness, longing for nothing to come between us and our Lord. Then Jesus takes us even further:

"Blessed are the merciful, for they will be shown mercy." – Matthew 5:7

This is where things get real. Mercy isn't just about feeling sorry for someone—it's about action. It's about choosing compassion over resentment, even when judgment seems justified. Mercy is for those who don't deserve it—because that's exactly what God has given us.

Core Message

One of my most difficult lessons in mercy happened while I was serving on the east side of Flint. I was working with a family that had taken in a few extra kids. Their situation was heartbreaking—poverty, abuse, and neglect surrounded them. I often felt helpless, wanting to fix it all but knowing I couldn't.

One day, I found out that three of these kids were sleeping on a hard wooden floor. No blankets. No pillows. Just the floor. My heart ached for them. I told my kids about the situation, and without hesitation, my oldest daughter—just 14 years old—decided to use part of her very first paycheck to buy them blankets and pillows. She didn't just feel bad; she did something.

Shortly after, I learned that Eastside Mission was giving away free mattresses. I asked if one was available, and they strapped it to the top of my car. I was so excited! I couldn't wait to see the kids' faces when they finally had a warm, soft place to sleep.

The next morning, I picked them up for church. Eagerly, I asked, "How did you sleep on your new mattress?"

Their answer crushed me.

"Oh, we didn't sleep on it. The adult in the house took it for herself."

I was livid. I didn't understand how someone could do that—how an adult could take from children who had nothing. I had worked so hard to help these kids, and now, it felt like my effort had been wasted.

That anger sat with me for days. I wrestled with it. And everywhere I turned, I kept running into the same verse:

"But go and learn what this means: 'I desire mercy, not sacrifice.' For I have not come to call the righteous, but sinners." – Matthew 9:13

I saw it in my Bible study. I heard it on the radio. I couldn't escape it. But I still didn't understand.

I worked at a mission. I served people in poverty every day. Wasn't I already showing mercy?

That's when the Holy Spirit gently opened my eyes.

I *had* been showing mercy—to the children. I loved them. I wanted to help them. But when it came to the adult in the home—the one who had taken what wasn't hers—I was only offering a *sacrifice*, not mercy. I was *tolerating* her, not loving her.

God wasn't just asking me to *give things*. He was asking me to *give mercy*.

What Mercy Really Means

Mercy isn't just about feeling bad for people who are easy to love. It's about choosing love when it's hard.

I had to face a hard truth: I had received *so much* mercy from God, yet I was withholding it from someone I thought didn't deserve it. But that's exactly the definition of mercy—it's undeserved.

So I prayed. I asked God to soften my heart. Instead of keeping my distance, I started talking to the adult in the home. I started praying for her. And as I did, something shifted. I saw her differently—not as the villain, but as a wounded child herself, just trying to survive.

Jesus didn't say, *"Blessed are those who show mercy when it makes sense."* He just said, *"Blessed are the merciful."* Period.

Living a Life of Mercy

Mercy is not a one-time act; it's a lifestyle.

Think about how much mercy *you* have been shown. The times God forgave you when you didn't deserve it. The times people gave you grace when they could have held a grudge.

Jesus told a story in Matthew 18 about a servant who was forgiven an enormous debt. But instead of extending the same mercy, he went out and harshly demanded repayment from someone who owed him far less. The master was furious:

"Shouldn't you have had mercy on your fellow servant just as I had on you?" – Matthew 18:33

That's the point. We don't give mercy because people deserve it. We give mercy because *we* didn't deserve it either.

Broken and Poured Out

Jesus is the ultimate example of mercy.

On the cross, He could have called down judgment on those who mocked Him. Instead, He said, *"Father, forgive them."*

That's mercy.

He was broken and poured out for *us*. And now, He calls us to be broken and poured out for others. To love when it's hard. To forgive when it's undeserved. To extend the same mercy we have freely received.

Jesus said that the merciful *will be shown mercy*. When we live this way, something amazing happens. Our hearts change. We start to look more like Jesus.

Mind Shift

☐ Who in your life needs mercy?

☐ Maybe it's someone who hurt you. Maybe it's someone who doesn't appreciate your kindness. Maybe it's someone you've judged rather than loved.

☐ How has God shown *you* mercy? How can you extend that mercy to someone else this week?

☐ Write it down. Pray about it. Let God shift your heart. Mercy isn't just a gift—it's a calling.

Your Mind Shift

_____

_____

_____

_____

_____

_____

Song Suggestion

"Broken and Spilled Out" by Steve Green

Closing Prayer

Father, thank You for Your mercy. I don't deserve it, yet You pour it out on me daily. Help me to be merciful, even when it's hard. Soften my heart toward those I struggle to love. Give me eyes to see people the way You do. Let me be broken and poured out, just like Jesus. May my life reflect Your mercy, so that others may come to know You. And may I give myself mercy on my journey of growth. In Jesus' name, Amen.

Day 69

Growing Your Roots

Lord as I go over the Mind Shifts that You have been teaching me, please grow them deep in my heart and mind. I want to see things like You. I want to think like You. Lord keep making me more and more like You. In Jesus Name. Amen.

1. Blessed are the Poor In Spirit; Foundation of Faith: Matthew 5:3 *"Blessed are the poor in spirit, for theirs is the kingdom of heaven."*

Your Mind Shift

_____

_____

_____

_____

2. Blessed are Those Who Mourn: Matthew 5:4 *"Blessed are those who mourn, for they shall be comforted."*

Your Mind Shift

_____

_____

_____

_____

3. Blessed are the Meek: Matthew 5:5 *"Blessed are the meek, for they shall inherit the earth."*

Your Mind Shift

_____

_____

_____

_____

4. Hungry and Thirsty: Matthew 5:6 *"Blessed are those who hunger and thirst for righteousness, for they shall be filled."*

Your Mind Shift

_____

_____

_____

_____

5. Blessed are the Merciful: – Matthew 5:7 "Blessed are the merciful, for they will be shown mercy."

Your Mind Shift

_____

_____

_____

_____

Closing Prayer

Lord God, thank You for Your Truth. Thank You that You gave us Your Word. Thank You that You didn't leave us to learn on our own but You have given us Your Holy Spirit to live in us and give us power. That Spirit of power, of CAN, show me that power within myself. In Jesus Name, Amen.

Day 70

Finishing the Week In Worship

Today we will go back to our thankful questions. If you feel led to go back to any of the previous devotionals and Mind Shifts, obey the Spirits leading.

Lord give us a thankful heart and eyes to see all that You have done for us and made known to us. In Jesus Name, Amen.

God I thank You for showing me that You are

_____

_____

_____

_____

God I thank You for what You have done

_____

_____

_____

_____

God I thank You for what I know You are doing

_____

_____

_____

_____

Go back to your favorite songs from this week and worship!!

Closing Prayer

Lord I am truely thankful for having You in my life. You fill me with love and forgive my shortcomings. Thank You for all of the blessings that I have listed above. You are so good to me. In Jesus Name. Amen.

Devotional

Pure in Heart

Focus Scripture

Matthew 5:8

"Blessed are the pure in heart, for they will see God."

Introduction

When we look at the Beatitudes in Matthew 5, there is a clear progression in spiritual growth. Each statement builds upon the last, revealing a journey of transformation in the believer's life. The phrase "Blessed are the pure in heart" is often tied to sanctification—the point in our walk with Christ when we desire more of Him and, in turn, surrender more of ourselves.

At the beginning of our journey with Jesus, we offer Him what we know to offer. When we first accept Him as Lord and Savior, we give Him our sins, our past mistakes, and the burdens that weigh us down. However, at that stage, we don't yet fully grasp what following Christ truly entails. We don't realize that He will ask us to trust Him not just with our failures but also with our hopes and dreams. We don't yet understand that walking with Him means laying down our fears and uncertainties, trusting that He will lead us in the right direction.

As we grow in faith and deepen our understanding of God's Word, we come to a pivotal moment of surrender. For me, there was a point where I realized I didn't just want to give God my sins—I wanted to give Him everything. My dreams, my relationships, my thoughts, my desires, my perspectives, and my future. I wanted every part of my life to be aligned with His will. This was a deeper surrender, a full offering of myself at the altar—not just my heart, but every fiber of my being.

In that moment of complete surrender, I prayed, "God, sanctify me. Make my desires like Yours. I trust You more than I trust myself." It was a defining moment—an act of trust that purified my heart in a way I had never experienced before. It didn't mean I had arrived at perfection, but I found that I no longer wrestled with the petty struggles that once consumed me. My focus shifted. My heart became attuned to God in a new way.

I was all in.

Core Message

The promise attached to this Beatitude is profound: "for they will see God." Those who are pure in heart will see Him—not just in eternity, but in their everyday lives. When we allow God to refine our hearts, our vision changes. We begin to see His hand at work in ways we never noticed before. We see Him in the beauty of His creation, in the kindness of others, and in the quiet whispers of His Spirit guiding us.

A pure heart is not about perfection, but about a posture of surrender. It is about coming to that place where we desire God more than anything else and trust Him with every part of who we are. And in doing so, we begin to truly see Him.

Mind Shift

Take a moment to reflect and write down your answers:

1. What areas of your life have you yet to fully surrender to God?

2. Have you reached a point where you desire not just to follow Christ but to give Him everything?

3. Ask God today to purify your heart and align your desires with His. Trust that in doing so, you will see Him more clearly than ever before.

Your Mind Shift

_____

_____

_____

_____

_____

_____

Song Suggestion

"Refiner" – Maverick City Music

Closing Prayer

Father, I desire a pure heart before You. I long to see You more clearly in my life. Show me the areas I still need to surrender and give me the faith to lay them down at Your feet. Sanctify me, Lord. Make my desires align with Yours, and help me to trust You fully. Thank You for the promise that those who are pure in heart will see You. I want to see You in every moment, in every decision, and in every season of my life. In Jesus' name, Amen.

Blessed Are the Peacemakers

Focus Scripture

Matthew 5:9

"Blessed are the peacemakers, for they will be called sons of God."

Introduction

When I think about a peacemaker, I don't just think of someone who avoids conflict or calms arguments. I think of someone who actively brings people into peace with God. The greatest peace we can ever know is the kind that reconciles us to our Creator.

Jesus' command in Matthew 28:19 says, "Therefore go and make disciples of all nations, baptizing them in the name of the Father and of the Son and of the Holy Spirit." That phrase "make disciples" doesn't just mean to instruct others; it means to be a disciple yourself. The way we lead others into peace with God is by first walking in that peace ourselves. Our own life is the loudest testimony of what it means to follow Jesus.

Core Message

I once heard a story about a pregnant pug that was hit by a car. The accident damaged her back legs so badly that they had to be amputated. Miraculously, she survived and went on to give birth to her puppies. As they grew, something unexpected happened—they began dragging their back legs, just like their mother. They had perfectly good legs, but because of what they had observed, they mimicked her movements.

That story nearly brought me to tears because it reminded me of the power of influence. Whether we realize it or not, people—our children, friends, and even strangers—are watching how we live. They learn what it means to follow Christ not just by what we say but by what we do.

Paul understood this when he said, "Follow my example, as I follow the example of Christ" (1 Corinthians 11:1). What if we lived in such a way that people could see Jesus in us? What if our faith, our repentance, and our obedience weren't just personal but were meant to lead others into peace with God?

A Peacemaker Is a Disciple-Maker

Being a peacemaker means helping others find reconciliation with God, and that is at the heart of making disciples. A disciple is simply a follower of Jesus, someone who walks with Him and seeks to become more like Him. But making disciples requires us to first be disciples. We cannot lead people into a peace that we do not carry ourselves.

I love how Paul describes this in 2 Corinthians 5:18-20:

"All this is from God, who reconciled us to himself through Christ and gave us the ministry of reconciliation: that God was reconciling the world to himself in Christ, not counting people's sins against them. And he has committed to us the message of reconciliation. We are therefore Christ's ambassadors, as though God were making his appeal through us."

God has given us the ministry of reconciliation—the privilege of helping others find peace with Him. We are not just recipients of salvation; we are called to share it. We are His ambassadors, representing Him in the world. Every word we speak, every action we take, and every moment of grace we extend can be an opportunity for someone else to see Christ in us.

But let's be real—our example will never be perfect. We will stumble. We will make mistakes. That's why one of the most powerful things we can do as disciples is model repentance. True repentance isn't just saying, "I'm sorry," but demonstrating real change. It means taking responsibility for our actions and allowing the Holy Spirit to transform us so that, more and more, we reflect Christ.

Mind Shift

- Being a peacemaker isn't just about avoiding conflict; it's about leading others into peace with God.

- Making disciples isn't just about teaching others; it's about living a life that others can follow.

- Our greatest testimony is not perfection but a life that continually seeks to reflect Jesus.

- Repentance isn't just an apology; it's changed behavior.

What is the Holy Spirit revealing to you about being a peacemaker? Write down your own mind shift below.

Your Mind Shift

_____

_____

_____

_____

_____

_____

Song Suggestion

"Jesus at the Center" – Israel Houghton

Closing Prayer

Father, I want to be a peacemaker, not just in the way I handle conflict, but in the way I lead others to You. Help me to be a disciple first, so that my life reflects Your love and truth. Let me be someone who makes peace by bringing others into a relationship with You. When I fail, help me to show genuine repentance so that others see Your grace at work in my life. May my life be a testimony of Your transforming power. In Jesus' name, Amen.

Devotional

Created to Be You (Part 1)

Focus Scripture

Ephesians 2:10 (NIV)

"For we are God's handiwork, created in Christ Jesus to do good works, which God prepared in advance for us to do."

Romans 5:2 (TLB)

"For because of our faith, he has brought us into this place of highest privilege where we now stand, and we confidently and joyfully look forward to actually becoming all that God has had in mind for us to be."

Introduction

I love thinking about how God made each of us completely unique. No two of us are exactly the same—not in our DNA, not in our fingerprints, not even in the way we laugh, think, or dream. That blows my mind! It's as if God looked at the world and said, "I'm

316

going to make her special. I'm going to put a part of Me inside of her that no one else has in quite the same way." And then He did.

But somewhere along the way, the world teaches us to blend in—to conform, to fit into categories and labels that were never meant for us. Instead of celebrating who God made us to be, we sometimes try to mold ourselves into what's expected, thinking that's where we'll find belonging. But have you ever noticed that the more we try to fit in, the more we lose the things that make us who we are?

Core Message

In *How Wolves Change Rivers*, a documentary about Yellowstone National Park, I learned how scientists reintroduced wolves after they had been gone for 70 years. Their absence had thrown everything off balance. The land had suffered. Without wolves to keep them in check, the deer and elk overgrazed, eating so much that the trees couldn't grow. As a result, the rivers became unstable, and life started to disappear.

But when the wolves returned, they did what they were designed to do—and because of that, everything changed. Trees started growing again. Birds returned. Beavers built their dams, and even the rivers became deeper and stronger.

God created the wolves with a specific purpose. They didn't have to try to be anything other than what they were made to be—and when they walked in that purpose, life flourished.

And isn't that just like us?

God created each of us with a purpose. He placed something inside of us that is meant to shape the world around us. But when we try to be something we're not—when we shrink, hide, or force ourselves into places that weren't meant for us—we lose the impact we were made to have.

God didn't make you to be like everyone else. He made you to be *you*. And when you fully step into who He created you to be, everything around you starts to shift. You bring life. You bring balance. You bring the presence of God into places that desperately need it.

That's what it means to joyfully and confidently step into all that God had in mind for you. Not striving. Not comparing. Just walking boldly in the person He made you to be.

Mind Shift

- God designed me with intention—I don't have to fit into someone else's mold.

- When I embrace my God-given uniqueness, I help bring life and balance to the world around me.

- The way God made me is on purpose, for a purpose.

Your Mind Shift

_____

_____

_____

_____

_____

_____

Song Suggestion

"Who You Say I Am" by Hillsong Worship

Closing Prayer

Father, thank You for creating me so intentionally. I don't want to waste my life trying to be someone You never designed me to be. Help me to trust that Your plan for me is good and that my uniqueness has a purpose. Show me how to walk boldly in the way You've made me. Let my life be one that brings life to the world around me, just like You intended. In Jesus Name, Amen.

Devotional

Trusting the Designer (Part 2)

Focus Scripture

Isaiah 55:8-9 (NIV)

*"For my thoughts are not your thoughts,
neither are your ways my ways," declares the
Lord. "As the heavens are higher than the
earth, so are my ways higher than your ways
and my thoughts than your thoughts."*

Proverbs 3:5-6 (NIV)

*"Trust in the Lord with all your heart and lean
not on your own understanding; in all your
ways submit to him, and he will make your
paths straight."*

Introduction

In the last devotional, we talked about how the wolves at
Yellowstone made an incredible impact just by being who they
were created to be. But there's something else that stood out to me

in that story: their presence didn't just restore order—it also created boundaries.

When the wolves returned, the deer and elk could no longer roam freely wherever they pleased. They had to move more often, giving trees and plants the time they needed to grow back. Those boundaries, though inconvenient for the animals, were what allowed life to flourish again.

And isn't that just like God's ways?

His design includes boundaries. His order of things may sometimes seem inconvenient or even outdated, but we don't have to understand it—we just need to trust Him.

Core Message

There are times when God's ways don't make sense to me. I like to have a plan, to see where I'm going, to know why things happen the way they do. But following God doesn't always come with explanations. Sometimes, He simply asks me to trust Him, even when I don't understand.

The wolves at Yellowstone didn't have to understand the science behind the changes they caused. They just had to be wolves. And we don't have to understand everything about God's ways—we just have to obey.

And when we do, we will be amazed at the beauty, depth, and strength that begin to grow in our lives. The surprises will come—not because we controlled the outcome, but because we let the Designer do what only He can do.

Mind Shift

God's ways are higher than mine—I don't have to understand everything to trust Him.

- Obedience brings blessings I may not see right away.

- Boundaries are not meant to hold me back, but to bring life and growth.

- God is the Designer. He knows what He's doing, and I can trust Him.

Your Mind Shift

_____

_____

_____

_____

_____

_____

_____

Song Suggestion

"Trust in You" by Lauren Daigle

Closing Prayer:

Father, there are so many times I don't understand what You're doing. Sometimes Your ways seem hard or confusing, and I struggle to trust. But I know that You are the Designer. You see the whole picture when I only see a tiny part. Help me to obey You even when I don't understand. Help me to trust that Your boundaries are for my good and that following You leads to life. Thank You for knowing what I need, even when I don't. In Jesus Name, Amen.

Devotional

The Lord is My Shepherd

Focus Scripture

Psalm 23:1

"The Lord is my shepherd, I lack nothing."

Introduction

My senior year of high school, I fell in love with Jesus—not in a surface-level way, but in a way that changed everything. It wasn't just about knowing who He was; I wanted to follow Him, to be close to Him, to live my life for Him.

Years later, when I started serving on the east side of Flint, I discovered something I never expected: a deep, lasting joy in following God's plan. It wasn't flashy or glamorous, but it filled me in a way that nothing else ever had. The more I walked with Him, the more I realized I wasn't missing out on anything—I was gaining everything.

I didn't have to chase after things to feel fulfilled. I lacked nothing because my Shepherd was taking care of me.

Core Message

David, the writer of *Psalm 23*, knew exactly what it meant to be a shepherd. He had spent years leading his father's sheep, making sure they were fed, protected, and safe. When predators came, he didn't run—he fought for them. He understood the responsibility, the sacrifice, and the love it took to care for those sheep.

So when he said, "The Lord is my shepherd," he wasn't being poetic; he was making a declaration. He was claiming God as his own personal Shepherd—the One he trusted to lead him, provide for him, and protect him.

A shepherd doesn't just throw food at his sheep and walk away. He stays with them. He calls them by name. He watches over them day and night. And if one wanders off, he doesn't just say, *Oh well, I've got plenty of others.* No—he goes after it. He searches for that one lost sheep until he finds it, carries it back, and rejoices that it's safe again.

That's who our Shepherd is.

The Fence of Protection

I once heard a story from Pastor Gary Loudermilk about his dog, Lucky. When Pastor Gary brought Lucky home, he set up a fenced yard with everything the dog could possibly need—food, water, toys, and even a little pool to splash in. It was a dog's dream.

But Lucky didn't see it that way. He kept jumping the fence. No matter how many times Pastor Gary fixed it, Lucky found a way out. He thought freedom was out there, beyond the fence, but he didn't realize that outside, he had no food, no water, and no protection.

How often do we act the same way?

God, our Shepherd, gives us everything we need. He leads us, provides for us, and sets up boundaries to keep us safe. But sometimes, we think we know better. We push against His guidance. We chase after things He never intended for us. And when we do, we find ourselves in places that leave us empty, unprotected, and searching for something to fill the void.

But here's the beautiful thing—our Shepherd doesn't give up on us. He doesn't leave us wandering. He comes after us, picks us up, and carries us home. And when we finally rest in His care, we realize we never really needed what was outside the fence. Everything we could ever want was with Him all along.

Mind Shift

- I don't have to search for satisfaction—my Shepherd provides everything I need.

- God's boundaries aren't to restrict me, but to protect and bless me.

- Even when I wander, He comes after me and leads me back to safety.

- True joy isn't found in chasing my own plans—it's found in following Him.

- I lack nothing because my Shepherd is always taking care of me.

Your Mind Shift

_____

_____

_____

_____

_____

Song Suggestion

"Steadfast by Firehouse

Closing Prayer

Lord, thank You for being my Shepherd. Thank You for leading me, protecting me, and providing everything I need. I confess that sometimes I act like Lucky, thinking I know better, chasing after things that won't satisfy. But You never stop pursuing me. You never stop loving me. Help me to trust You, to follow You, and to rest in the truth that I lack nothing in Your care. In Jesus' name, Amen.

Devotional

Feasting at the Table

Focus Scripture

Psalm 23:5

"You prepare a table before me in the presence of my enemies. You anoint my head with oil; my cup overflows."

Introduction

There's something so powerful about the image in *Psalm 23* of God preparing a table for us—not just anywhere, but in the presence of our enemies. It's a reminder that He has already provided everything we need to be sustained today. Right there, in the middle of whatever we're facing—whether it's doubt, discouragement, stress, or exhaustion—He invites us to sit and feast.

But here's the thing: a feast doesn't nourish you if you don't stop and eat.

Core Message

I believe one of the most beneficial things we can do is slow down in the morning to sit at that banquet table and take in what God has prepared—to fill up on His truth, His promises, and His presence before we step into the day.

Because when we don't? We walk around empty.

And when we're empty, we start looking for something—*anything*—to feed us. Instead of walking into our day confident that we are loved, chosen, and enough, we start searching for affirmation from people. Instead of standing firm in God's strength, we feel inadequate and unsure of ourselves. Instead of being filled with peace, we scramble for quick fixes that leave us unsatisfied.

It's like skipping breakfast and then craving donuts all morning. When you start the day hungry, your body reaches for whatever is easiest, even if it's not what you actually need. But when you take the time to eat something real, something nourishing, your body is sustained.

God's table works the same way. When we stop and receive from Him first, we walk into the day already full. We aren't looking for scraps from the world because we've already feasted on what truly satisfies.

The Table is Set

The Lord isn't haphazard about this table—He has prepared it. He knows exactly what we need today—peace for anxious thoughts, courage for difficult moments, strength for heavy burdens. And He doesn't just give us a little bit. Our cup overflows.

We see this same invitation in *Isaiah*:

"Come, all you who are thirsty, come to the waters; and you who have no money, come, buy and eat! Come, buy wine and milk without money and without cost." – *Isaiah 55:1*

God's table isn't just for the days when we feel worthy or strong. It's for us on our weakest days, our empty days, our struggling days. He calls us to come and be filled—not because we've earned it, but because He loves us.

There's a quote by Corrie ten Boom that fits so well:

"Don't pray when you feel like it. Have an appointment with the Lord and keep it. A man is powerful on his knees."

She understood that sitting at God's table isn't just a good idea—it's a necessity. If we don't make time for Him first, everything else suffers.

Mind Shift

- God has already provided everything I need for today—I just need to receive it.

- If I start my day full, I won't search for empty things to sustain me.

- My Shepherd knows what I need before I even step into my day.

- Spending time with God first isn't a chore; it's the feast that strengthens me.

- I don't have to rely on people or circumstances to fill me—I am already full in Him.

Your Mind Shift

_____

_____

_____

_____

_____

_____

Song Suggestion

"Fill Me Up" by Tasha Cobb

Closing Prayer

Lord, thank You for always preparing a table for me. I know that You have everything I need, but sometimes I rush into my day without stopping to receive it. Help me to slow down and feast on Your truth before I step out into the world. Fill me so completely that I don't go searching for scraps elsewhere. I want to walk in the confidence that I am loved, chosen, and equipped for whatever today holds. In Jesus' name, Amen.

Devotional

He is with You

Focus Scripture

Psalm 23:4

"Even though I walk through the valley of the shadow of death, I will fear no evil, for You are with me; Your rod and Your staff, they comfort me."

Introduction

Psalm 23 has been one of my lifelines. God has used it in so many ways—to feed my soul when I felt empty, to remind me of His presence when I felt surrounded, and to restore me when I was weary.

Core Message

There was a season in my life when the weight of busyness pressed down on me. My mind felt like a whirlwind—constantly moving but never settling. To quiet the noise, I started a routine of walking up and down my driveway each morning, trying to still my thoughts and simply be in God's presence.

Every morning, I would walk. And every morning, I would recite *Psalm 23*. It became my rhythm, my anchor, my reminder of who God is.

Then one day, I felt especially heavy. Loneliness was creeping in, and I couldn't seem to shake it. I went outside for my usual walk, reciting the words that had become so familiar.

But this time, the Holy Spirit nudged me.

"You're missing something."

That thought seemed silly. I had been saying Psalm 23 for months—surely, I wasn't leaving anything out. But I knew if God was pointing something out, He was right.

After I finished my walk, I went inside, grabbed my Bible, and read through Psalm 23 aloud. And there it was. The words I had unknowingly skipped.

"For You are with me."

Tears welled up in my eyes. That was exactly what I needed at that moment. The God of the universe had taken the time to get my attention, to remind me of something I had forgotten in my heart, even though my mouth had been saying the words for months.

He is with me.

Never Alone

As a Christ-follower, there is one thing I never have to be again—alone.

The Lord has been my best friend for over 33 years. He is the One I talk to in my car, the One I whisper to in my room, the One who hears the prayers I can't even form into words. He is not distant. He is near.

There is a security that comes with knowing He will never leave me or forsake me. He knows me better than anyone ever could—yet He chooses to stay. He chooses to be with me.

And He chooses to be with you too.

Mind Shift

- God is not just present when I feel Him—He is always with me.

- Even in my loneliest moments, I am not alone.

- The security of His presence is unshakable.

Your Mind Shift

_____

_____

_____

_____

_____

_____

Song Suggestion

You Are With Me by Mandisa

Closing Prayer

Father, thank You for being with me. In every season, in every valley, in every joy, You are here. Forgive me for the times I forget Your presence and try to walk alone. Help me to recognize that I am never by myself because You are always near. Teach me to rest in the security of knowing You see me, hear me, and love me. In Jesus' Name, Amen.

Day 76

Growing Your Roots

Lord today as I continue to renew my mind, please transform me. I want to grow and become more and more like You. I ask You to please help me dig in and fight for Truth to win in my mind and in my heart. Lord help me shine Your Light to the world so that others may see my life and find their way to You. Show me where I need to grow. I am Your servant and I am listening. In Jesus Name, Amen.

1. Pure in Heart: Matthew 5:8 – "Blessed are the pure in heart, for they will see God."

Your Mind Shift

_____

_____

_____

_____

2. Blessed Are The Peacemakers: Matthew 5:9 *"Blessed are the peacemakers, for they will be called sons of God."*

Your Mind Shift

_____

_____

_____

_____

3. The Lord is My Shepherd: Psalms 23:1 *"The Lord is my shepherd, I lack nothing."*

Your Mind Shift

_____

_____

_____

_____

4. Feasting At The Table: Psalms 23:5 *"You prepare a table before me in the presence of my enemies. You anoint my head with oil; my cup overflows."*

Your Mind Shift

_____

_____

_____

_____

5. He is With You: Psalms 23:4 *"Even though I walk through the valley of the shadow of death, I will fear no evil, for You are with me; Your rod and Your staff, they comfort me."*

Hopefully you are learning a new habit of not just learning, but relearning and relearning new mind shifts. After you reread the devotional that you need to soak in today, write down any new information that you want to be able to look back at.

_____

_____

_____

_____

Closing Prayer

Lord, please keep me pliable and teachable as I learn these new mind shifts. Keep me humble, realizing that I am still learning just like those around me. Feed me Holy Spirit until I overflow. Thank You for never leaving me alone, for allowing me to feast at Your table every day. I have You and that means that I have all that I need. I believe You. In Jesus Name. Amen.

Day 77

Finishing the Week In Worship

This is the day that the Lord has made, let us rejoice and be glad in it. Today I would like you to go back and worship with the songs that have meant the most to you. As the Holy Spirit to fill you with the truth in the words you are singing. Remember our praise is the water our enemies drown in.

Write the name of the song and the way it speaks to you below.

_____

_____

_____

_____

Closing prayer

Lord, we worship You because of who You are. In Jesus Name. Amen.

Devotional

Rescued by the Shepherd

Focus Scripture

Psalm 23:4

"Even though I walk through the valley of the shadow of death, I will fear no evil, for You are with me; Your rod and Your staff, they comfort me."

Introduction

Psalm 23 is one of those scriptures I have heard preached countless times, but there was one sermon, over a decade ago, that stayed with me. The preacher was explaining the role of a shepherd's rod and staff, and something deep inside me changed as I listened.

Before that, I had always assumed the rod was for discipline. I imagined God using it to get me back in line. That thought never brought me comfort.

But then I learned the truth.

A shepherd doesn't use his rod to harm his sheep—he uses it to protect them.

The rod is a weapon, wielded against anything that threatens the flock. Wolves, lions, and thieves all know the force of a shepherd's rod. When danger comes, the shepherd doesn't hesitate—he swings with strength and precision, driving the enemy away.

When I understood that, it brought me comfort and confidence.

Now, when I recite *Psalm 23*, I picture my Shepherd standing over me, rod in hand, fiercely defending me. I imagine Him striking down every attack the enemy sends my way.

Sometimes, I say it out loud:

"Your rod is beating off discouragement."

"Your rod is beating off despair."

"Your rod is beating off fear."

"Your rod is beating off anxiety."

I don't have to fight alone. My Shepherd is fighting for me.

That realization doesn't just comfort me—it strengthens me.

Core Message

Then, there's the staff.

Unlike the rod, which is used for battle, the staff is a tool of guidance, rescue, and connection. It is long and slender, with a hook at the end, and the shepherd uses it in many ways to care for his sheep.

One of the most powerful images of the staff is its role in rescue. In the wilderness, where shepherds lead their flocks, the terrain is rough and uneven. There are deep cracks and ravines where a sheep can slip and fall, unable to climb out on its own. When that happens, the shepherd takes his staff, turns it upside down, and carefully lowers the hook beneath the sheep's belly, lifting it back to safety.

I cannot tell you how many times I have been that sheep.

How many times have I wandered too close to the edge, convinced I knew what I was doing, only to find myself stuck in a place I couldn't escape? How many times have I chased after something I thought I wanted, only to realize too late that I had fallen into a pit?

And then there are the times when I didn't even get myself there.

Someone else pushed me. A harsh word, a betrayal, a situation I never asked for—suddenly, I was down in the crevice, lost, hurt, and unsure how to climb out.

But my Shepherd saw me.

He didn't leave me there, telling me to figure it out on my own. He reached for me.

With His staff, He lifted me up, dusted me off, and set me back on solid ground.

And that's not all the staff does.

The shepherd also uses it to gently guide the sheep, nudging them in the right direction when they begin to stray. He doesn't use force or fear—just a gentle, steady touch, keeping them close, keeping them safe.

That is the heart of Jesus.

He rescues.

He leads.

He stays close.

Rescued Again

The greatest comfort I know is this: Jesus will always come for me.

There is no pit too deep.

No mistake too big.

No failure too far gone.

He traded heaven to have me again.

That line from *Touch the Sky* undoes me every time. The King of everything left His throne, His glory, His perfect place in heaven—just to come and rescue me. Again and again.

And He will do the same for you.

If you feel stuck in a place you can't climb out of, take heart. Your Shepherd is already reaching for you.

Let Him lift you back up.

Let Him lead you.

Let Him remind you that you are never out of His sight.

That is the comfort of the rod and the staff.

Mind Shift

- God is protecting me.

- When I fall, Jesus is coming to rescue me.

- I am never too far gone for my Shepherd to reach me.

Your Mind Shift

_____

_____

_____

_____

_____

_____

Songs Suggestion

- *Touch the Sky* by Hillsong UNITED

- *Rescue* by Lauren Daigle

Closing Prayer

Lord, thank You for being my Shepherd. Thank You for fighting for me when the enemy comes against me. Thank You for rescuing me when I fall. Thank You for guiding me, even when I don't realize I need it. I don't always understand why I end up in certain places, but I trust that You see me and that You will never leave me there. Help me to lean on You and find comfort in knowing that You are always near. In Jesus' Name, Amen.

Devotional

Resting in the Unforced Rhythms of Grace

Focus Scripture

Matthew 11:28-30 (MSG)

"Are you tired? Worn out? Burned out on religion? Come to me. Get away with me and you'll recover your life. I'll show you how to take a real rest. Walk with me and work with me—watch how I do it. Learn the unforced rhythms of grace. I won't lay anything heavy or ill-fitting on you. Keep company with me and you'll learn to live freely and lightly."

Introduction

Lately, this verse has been everywhere in my life. I memorized it not long ago, and since then, it keeps showing up in conversations, sermons, and quiet moments with God. It's as if He's been gently nudging me, saying, Pay attention. This is for you. And the more I sit with it, the more I realize how much I need it.

The phrase that stands out to me most is "learn the unforced rhythms of grace." It reminds me of *Galatians 5:25*, which says to "keep in step with the Spirit." For a long time, God has given me the image of us dancing through life together. But the reality is, I don't always know the steps. Life changes, the rhythm shifts, and suddenly, I feel completely off balance.

Yet, God isn't frustrated with me when I stumble. He isn't impatient when I miss a step. Instead, He holds my hands and reminds me, *I know the dance. You're learning. Just stay close to Me.*

Core Message

Learning the unforced rhythms of grace isn't just about receiving grace—it's about giving it, too. I want to be someone who looks at others with kindness, believing the best about them. I don't know their full story. I don't know their struggles or the weight they're carrying.

Just as God is gracious with me, I am called to extend that same grace to those around me.

What Are You Carrying That's Not Yours?

The second part of this passage that speaks deeply to me is this: *"I won't lay anything heavy or ill-fitting on you."*

I've had seasons where I felt overwhelmed, burdened by things that seemed too much to bear. But this verse tells me that if something feels crushing, it's not from God. That doesn't mean He won't call me to hard things. It means I was never meant to do them alone.

If I'm feeling weighed down, I have to ask myself:

- Am I trying to fix something I have no control over?

- Am I carrying someone else's emotional weight, believing it's my job to solve their problems?

- Am I placing expectations on myself that God never asked of me?

Jesus tells us to be yoked to Him—to walk with Him, to let Him carry the load. If something feels unbearable, it's either because I'm trying to carry it alone or because I'm holding onto something that was never mine to begin with.

I don't have to fix everything.

I don't have to control everything.

I don't have to hold it all together.

Jesus offers me rest—not just a break, but a deep, soul-level rest. He wants me to breathe, to trust Him, to let go of the things that are weighing me down.

Mind Shift

- Grace isn't just something I receive; it's something I give.

- If it feels heavy and ill-fitting, it's not from God.

- I am only responsible for what God has called *me* to do, not for controlling others.

- True rest comes from being yoked with Jesus, not from working harder.

Your Mind Shift

_____

_____

_____

_____

_____

_____

Song Suggestion

"Carry me" by Steve Camp

Closing Prayer

Jesus, I come to You, tired and worn out from carrying things You never asked me to carry. I lay them at Your feet. Teach me how to dance in step with You, to follow Your lead, to move in the unforced rhythms of Your grace. Help me to release control, to let go of what is heavy and ill-fitting, and to find true rest in You. Fill me with grace—not just to receive it but to extend it to others. I choose to trust You. I choose to walk freely and lightly with You. In Jesus Name, Amen.

Don't Leave Without Your Plunder

Focus Scripture

---

2 Chronicles 20:25

"So Jehoshaphat and his men went to carry off their plunder, and they found among them a great amount of equipment and clothing, and also articles of value—more than they could take away. There was so much plunder that it took three days to collect it."

Introduction

This story in 2 Chronicles 20 gets me every time. If you've never read it, go back and soak it in. Three armies came against God's people, and King Jehoshaphat did exactly what I wish I always did first—he sought the Lord. And what did God say?

"Do not be afraid or discouraged because of this vast army. For the battle is not yours, but God's... Take up your positions; stand

firm and see the deliverance the Lord will give you... Do not be
afraid; do not be discouraged. Go out to face them tomorrow, and
the Lord will be with you."

— 2 Chronicles 20:15-17

Core Message

Imagine that. You're outnumbered, unprepared, and terrified. But instead of giving you a battle strategy, God says, "Take up your positions, stand firm, and see the deliverance of the Lord."

And as they praised their way to the battlefield, God caused their enemies to turn on each other. By the time Judah arrived, it was over. They didn't even have to lift a sword.

That alone would have been enough. But then comes verse 25— the part is a new truth for me. Not only did God win the battle for them, but He left them with more than they could carry.

Three whole days of collecting the spoils of war.

The very enemy that came to destroy them ended up supplying them.

God didn't just protect them. He blessed them.

And that's when it hit me—how often do I leave the battlefield without my plunder?

What's Your Plunder?

I don't ask this lightly.

For a long time, I couldn't see any plunder in my battle.

When I was in my emotionally abusive marriage, I only saw destruction. It wrecked me in ways I still don't have words for. Shame wrapped itself around me like a heavy coat. Fear whispered that I would never be whole again.

And the enemy knew exactly how to keep me bound.

He lined up his attacks with my weakest areas. I was already struggling with my self-worth, and he used the very Word of God against me—twisting Scripture to make me feel like I was failing as a wife, a mother, and a woman of faith.

"You're not submissive enough."

"You're not a good wife."

"You're failing at marriage again."

And the worst part? I believed it.

I stayed longer than I should have—not just because I wanted to honor God, but because I was terrified of failing. I didn't want to admit that this marriage, the one I prayed so hard for, was falling apart.

And little by little, I lost myself.

I can still remember the way my heart would race as I pulled into the driveway. The panic that set in before I even walked through the door. The deep, unshakable exhaustion from fighting a battle I didn't even know how to win.

But God.

God came for me in that dark place. He didn't just pull me out— He made sure I didn't leave empty-handed.

He gave me light when I was drowning in darkness.

He gave me a safe place to heal when I felt like I had nowhere to turn.

He gave me courage when I was paralyzed by fear.

And the biggest plunder of all?

He made me an overcomer.

I didn't just walk away from that battle—I walked away stronger.

I walked away knowing I can survive things I never thought I could.

I walked away with a new fire in my soul and a deeper compassion for women who are still trapped.

And now? I'm taking back everything the enemy stole from me.

I will not walk around clothed in shame.

I will not let fear silence me.

I will not let the battle break me.

I don't always *feel* like her, but I AM HER.

- Overcomer

- Mighty warrior

- Child of God

What the enemy meant to destroy me only made me stronger.

Mind Shift

What about you? Have you taken your plunder?

- What has God revealed to you about who He is through your battles?

- What has He shown you about who you are?

- What do you have now that you didn't have before?

- What weapons has He placed in your hands?

Write it down. Speak it out loud. Take your plunder.

Your Mind Shift

_____

_____

_____

_____

_____

_____

Songs Suggestion

- "Overcomer" by Mandisa

- "Take It All Back" by Tauren Wells

Turn these up loud. Let them remind you of who you are.

Closing Prayer

Father, thank You for fighting for me. Thank You for never leaving me in the battle alone. I don't want to just survive my struggles— I want to come out stronger. Help me to see the plunder in my pain. Help me to recognize the ways You have equipped me through every hardship. I don't want to leave the battlefield empty-handed. I am taking back everything the enemy stole. My joy. My confidence. My identity. My peace. And I refuse to walk in anything less than the full victory You have given me. In Jesus Name, Amen.

Devotional

Letting Go to Move Forward

Focus Scripture

Deuteronomy 20:19

"When you lay siege to a city for a long time, fighting against it to capture it, do not destroy its trees by putting an ax to them, because you can eat their fruit. Do not cut them down. Are the trees people, that you should besiege them?"

Introduction

The battle had been long, exhausting, and full of lessons I never expected to learn. I had fought through struggles, disappointments, and heartaches, trusting God to see me through. Finally, the breakthrough came. The season shifted, and I could feel God leading me forward.

But instead of feeling free, I felt anxious. I wasn't weighed down by the battle itself—I was worried about what others would think of me if I truly stepped into this new season. Would they misunderstand my choices? Would they think I was being distant or ungrateful? Some relationships had been part of my life for so long, but deep down, I knew they weren't growing with me.

That's when the Holy Spirit brought me to *Deuteronomy 20:19-20.* In this passage, God instructs Israel on what to do when taking new territory. He tells them not to destroy fruit-bearing trees because they will be needed for nourishment, but trees that do not produce fruit can be cut down.

Core Message

I realized God was showing me something deeper. Not everything from my last season needed to come with me. Some things—the wisdom I had gained, the maturity I had developed—were fruit-bearing. They would sustain me in the future. But other things— the relationships that no longer grew, the fears I had learned to live with—needed to be left behind. Holding on to them would only keep me looking back when God was calling me forward.

Letting go doesn't mean the past wasn't valuable. It simply means that what served its purpose in one season may not be necessary for the next. God isn't asking us to abandon everything, but He is calling us to discern what should remain and what should be released.

That's why Paul reminds us:

"But one thing I do: Forgetting what is behind and straining toward what is ahead, I press on toward the goal to win the prize for which God has called me heavenward in Christ Jesus."

—Philippians 3:13-14

God is doing a new thing. If we stay too focused on the past, we will miss it.

"Forget the former things; do not dwell on the past. See, I am doing a new thing! Now it springs up; do you not perceive it? I am making a way in the wilderness and streams in the wasteland."

—Isaiah 43:18-19

I had to ask myself: Was I holding on to something that was keeping me from stepping fully into God's next for me? Was I afraid of disappointing people more than I was afraid of disobeying God?

Maybe you're facing a similar choice. Maybe God is shifting you into a new season, but you feel hesitant to move forward because of what others might think. It's hard to release what we've known, but freedom comes when we trust that God will sustain us with what truly matters.

Mind Shift

- Not everything from my last season belongs in my next.

- Letting go is not losing; it's making room for what God has ahead.

- What bore fruit then may not bear fruit now, and that's okay.

- Growth requires pruning. It's time to release what no longer nourishes me.

- What is distracting me from the new thing God is doing in and through me?

- Am I more concerned about what people think than what God is calling me to do?

Your Mind Shift

_____

_____

_____

_____

_____

_____

_____

Quote

"You can't start the next chapter of your life if you keep re-reading the last one." —Unknown

Song Suggestion

"New" by Lauren Daigle

Closing Prayer

Father, I trust You with my next season. Help me to discern what to keep and what to let go of. Give me courage to release what no longer bears fruit and to hold onto the lessons, wisdom, and relationships You want to sustain me. I don't want to stay stuck in what was when You are calling me into something new. And Lord, help me not to be afraid of what others think. My obedience to You matters more than their approval. Lead me forward with open hands and an expectant heart. In Jesus' name, Amen.

Devotional

Step Out in Faith

Focus Scripture

Matthew 14:28-29 (NIV)

"Lord, if it's you," Peter replied, "tell me to come to you on the water." "Come," he said. Then Peter got down out of the boat, walked on the water and came toward Jesus."

Introduction

The *Kids Count* Building was a six-month project—six months of planning, fundraising, working, and trusting that God would see it through. Some days were exciting, full of visible progress and encouragement. Other days, like this one, tested my faith in ways I hadn't expected.

Core Message

On this particular workday, we had a crew of volunteers ready to make big strides. Someone had generously loaned their trailer so I could pick up drywall and insulation, and I rushed to get everything from Lowe's early that morning. My goal was simple: get the materials there as quickly as possible so the team could have the full day to work.

When we arrived at the site, the volunteers started unloading. One of the guys pulled out some drywall and asked, "What thickness is this?"

I told him, and he frowned. "This isn't going to work. It won't meet code."

My stomach dropped. I had bought the wrong drywall.

Trying not to panic, we moved the drywall aside and started unloading the insulation. Then another guy stopped and checked the label. "Uh... this is the wrong kind of insulation."

At that moment, I felt myself sinking. The faith that had carried me into this project—the boldness that had given me the confidence to start—felt like it was slipping away. How could I have messed this up so badly? People had trusted me. They had given their time and money to this vision, and here I was, completely unqualified and overwhelmed.

This was just one of many workdays, but on this particular day, my confidence wavered. The wind and waves of doubt and discouragement came crashing in—much like they did for Peter when he stepped out onto the water.

Peter's Sinking Moment

Peter knew what it was like to step out in faith and suddenly feel like he was sinking.

At first, Peter had the courage to leave the boat. That alone was incredible—no other disciple even tried. He believed that if Jesus was walking on water, then as His disciple, he could do the same. And for a few miraculous steps, he did.

But then the reality of the storm hit. The wind was loud. The waves were high. The impossible suddenly felt impossible again. He took his eyes off Jesus, fear took over, and he began to sink.

I get that. Maybe you do too.

Maybe you've stepped out in faith—started something new, taken a risk, followed God's call—but now, things aren't going the way you thought they would. The wind is howling, and doubt is creeping in.

But here's the good news: when Peter started to sink, he called out to Jesus, and Jesus immediately reached out and caught him.

Not after a long pause.

Not after letting Peter struggle for a while.

Immediately.

That's our Jesus. He doesn't let us drown. He is always right there, ready to pull us up.

God's Faithfulness Through the Process

That day at the worksite, I wanted to quit. I wanted to sit down in the middle of the mess and cry. The doubts were loud:

You aren't qualified for this.

You should have let someone else handle it.

You're wasting people's time.

But in the middle of my frustration, God reminded me that my faith wasn't in my ability to get everything right—it was in Him. He didn't call me to this because I had all the answers. He called me because He wanted to show me His faithfulness and that He can use anyone.

So, I swallowed my embarrassment, admitted my mistakes, and we made a plan. We returned the materials, got the right ones, and by the grace of God, we still got some work done that day.

And in the bigger picture? The Kids Count Building was completed. Today, it's still being used for kids' church. That day wasn't the end of the story. It was just one moment in a long process of learning to trust God through every step.

And that's what faith looks like. It's not perfect. It's not about getting everything right. It's about stepping out, trusting God, and knowing that even when we start to sink, He is always there to catch us.

Mind Shift

- Faith isn't about getting everything right; it's about trusting the One who called you.

- You don't have to have all the answers—just the courage to keep going.

- Even when your faith wavers, God remains faithful.

- The storms will come, but they don't define your journey— *Jesus does.*

What step of faith is God asking you to take right now? What fears are trying to hold you back?

Your Mind Shift

_____

_____

_____

_____

Song Suggestion

Oceans (Where Feet May Fail) – Hillsong United

Closing Prayer

Lord, I don't want to let fear or mistakes keep me from stepping out in faith. I know You have called me, and I trust that You will equip me. When the storms come, help me keep my eyes on You. When I start to sink, remind me that You are always near, always ready to lift me up. Strengthen my faith, Lord, and help me walk boldly wherever You lead. In Jesus' name, Amen.

Day 83

Growing Your Roots

1. Rescued by the Shepherd: Psalm 23:4 *"Even though I walk through the valley of the shadow of death, I will fear no evil, for You are with me; Your rod and Your staff, they comfort me."*

Your Mind Shift

_____

_____

_____

_____

_____

2. Resting in the Unforced Rhythms of Grace: Matthew 11:28-30 (The Message) *"Are you tired? Worn out? Burned out on religion? Come to me. Get away with me and you'll recover your life. I'll show you how to take a real rest. Walk with me and work with me—watch how I do it. Learn the unforced rhythms of grace. I won't lay anything heavy or ill-fitting on you. Keep company with me and you'll learn to live freely and lightly."*

Your Mind Shift

_____

_____

_____

_____

3. Don't Leave Without Your Plunder: 2 Chronicles 20:25 "So Jehoshaphat and his men went to carry off their plunder, and they found among them a great amount of equipment and clothing, and also articles of value—more than they could take away. There was so much plunder that it took three days to collect it."

Your Mind Shift

_____

_____

_____

_____

4. Letting Go To Move Forward: Duet 20:19 *"When you lay siege to a city for a long time, fighting against it to capture it, do not destroy its trees by putting an ax to them, because you can eat their fruit. Do not cut them down. Are the trees people, that you should besiege them?"*

Your Mind Shift

_____

_____

_____

_____

5. Step Out In Faith: Matthew 14:28-29 *Lord, if it's you," Peter replied, "tell me to come to you on the water." "Come," he said. Then Peter got down out of the boat, walked on the water and came toward Jesus."*

Your Mind Shift

_____

_____

_____

_____

Look back at the devotional that the Holy Spirit is drawing you to from this last week or any week. Ask the Lord to speak to you. Write any new mind shifts down.

_____

_____

_____

_____

Day 84

Finishing the Week In Worship

Yes Lord! Yes Lord! You have made it through 84 days, 12 weeks of intentionally getting into Gods Word and asking Him to transform your mind. Today, look back at all the mind shifts and stop wherever the Lord leads you. Hopefully you have gotten pretty good at holding onto the mind shifts that the Lord has shown you. My prayer is that you will use this devotional even after today to look at those mind shifts and be reminded of God's Truth. And the most awesome thing is when we look back at them and see how much God has grown us.

Write down any page numbers that want to easily access.

_____

_____

_____

_____

_____

_____

_____

_____

_____

_____

Closing Prayer

Lord God! My God! Thee True God that holds the stars in place and knows my name, I love You. Keep me close Lord, grow my roots deep in Your Love for me. May Your Love keep me steady when my world is shaking. Lord keep my mind fixed on You and to continue to grow deeper and deeper in my relationship with You. May Your Love and Your Truth change the way I see people and see myself. As I try my very best today, may I make You smile. I am Your Servant Lord and so thankful to be. In Jesus Name. Amen.

Devotional

The Belt of Truth: Holding Me Together

Focus Scripture

Ephesians 6:14 (NIV)

"Stand firm then, with the belt of truth buckled around your waist, with the breastplate of righteousness in place."

Introduction

Tonight, I wrestled. Hard.

The enemy wasn't subtle. It felt like an all-day battle, a relentless attack on my thoughts. I knew the lies weren't true, but that didn't stop them from coming. No matter how many times I pushed them away, another one would sneak in. The cycle was exhausting.

Core Message

I prayed, asking the Lord how He wanted me to finish this devotional book. I wanted to end strong, but I didn't feel strong. Then the Holy Spirit whispered, *Finish with the devotional you need to hear tonight.*

That's when He led me to Ephesians 6—the armor of God.

At first, I wasn't sure which piece of armor to focus on. But as I kept reading, my eyes locked onto the belt of truth. And I knew. That's what I needed tonight. That's what had been holding me together all along.

I remembered something from an inner healing prayer session. The leader had asked me to ask the Lord what my armor looked like. I had never done anything like that before, but as I sat quietly and listened, I saw it.

My belt of truth wasn't just a belt. It had gemstones hanging down, like charms on a bracelet. And each gemstone represented a promise—truths that God had spoken to me. They weren't just words. They weren't just verses. They were holding me together.

His Promises Pulled Me Back Together

As I sat there, feeling the weight of the day pressing in, the Holy Spirit began reminding me of the very promises we have talked about in this devotional book. These were the truths I had learned, the mind shifts I had written down, the moments when His Word had steadied me before. And tonight, as I wrote them down again, I could feel that belt of truth pulling me back together—wrapping around me with a calm peace and a steady assurance that He's got me.

I needed to remember that the Lord is my Shepherd, and because of that, I have everything I need. Even when my emotions try to convince me otherwise, I am never lacking—because He is my provider, my protector, and the One who leads me.

I needed to remember that, just like Peter, when I feel like I'm sinking under the weight of my worries, I can cry out to Jesus, and He will immediately reach for me. He doesn't hesitate. He doesn't wait to see if I can pull myself together. He lifts me up the moment I call His name.

I needed to remember that I don't have to carry my anxieties alone. He has invited me to bring them to Him with thanksgiving, and in exchange, He gives me peace—real peace, the kind that guards my heart and mind when everything else feels chaotic.

I needed to remember that my mind doesn't have to be a battlefield for the enemy. I can choose to think about what is true, noble, right, pure, lovely, and praiseworthy. I don't have to dwell on the lies or the fears. I can fix my thoughts on Him.

And as these promises filled my heart again, I felt the difference. The weight lifted. The enemy's lies lost their grip. His truth had pulled me back together.

Mind Shift

God's promises aren't just something we read once and forget. They are meant to be worn, carried, spoken, and believed. They are the belt of truth that holds us together when the enemy wants to unravel us.

- When your thoughts feel overwhelming, remember: God's truth is stronger than the enemy's lies.

- When fear tries to take over, remind yourself: God's promises are my anchor.

- When you feel like you're falling apart, declare: His truth is holding me together.

What promises has God spoken to you in this devotional journey? Write them down. Hold onto them. Let them become part of your belt of truth.

Your Mind Shift

_____

_____

_____

_____

_____

_____

Song Suggestion

"Truth I'm Standing On" by Leanna Crawford

Closing Prayer

Father, thank You for Your truth that holds me together when everything else feels like it's falling apart. When the enemy comes at me with lies, remind me of the promises You have spoken. Let them be the belt of truth that secures me, the foundation that steadies me, the weapon that silences the enemy.

I pray that every promise You have revealed in this devotional book would not just be something we read but something that becomes a part of us. Let these mind shifts stay with us, reminding us of who You are and who we are in You.

When the enemy tries to unravel me, pull me back together with Your truth.

I trust You, Lord. I stand firm in You. In Jesus' name, Amen.

And that is how we finish this devotional journey—standing firm, held together by His truth. These promises aren't just for a moment; they are for a lifetime. Keep them close. Wear them. Let them hold you together.